FOR GOD'S SAKE SHOOT STRAIGHT

FOR GOD'S SAKE SHOOT STRAIGHT

The Story of the Court Martial
and Execution of
Temporary Sub-Lieutenant Edwin Leopold Arthur Dyett
Nelson Battalion, 63rd (RN) Division
during the First World War

BY
LEONARD SELLERS

LEO COOPER
LONDON

This book is dedicated to the memory of Edwin Dyett
and all the victims of executions during the First World
War:
the condemned, their families and friends, and those
charged with their execution.

First published in Great Britain in 1995 by
LEO COOPER
190 Shaftesbury Avenue, London WC2H 8JL
an imprint of
Pen & Sword Books Ltd,
47 Church Street, Barnsley, South Yorkshire S70 2AS
Copyright © Leonard Sellers 1995

A CIP catalogue record for this book is available
from the British Library

ISBN 0 85052 470 9

Typeset in 11 on 12pt Linotype Sabon
by Phoenix Typesetting, Ilkley, West Yorkshire

Printed by
Redwood Books, Trowbridge, Wiltshire.

Contents

Acknowledgments

I wish to thank the following for their help and support. Without them this book would not have been possible:–

Miss Pat Andrew; His Honour Judge Anthony Babington; Captain J.F.T. Bayliss; P. Beaven; Judith M. Blacklaw; Miss C.M Blair; the British Library; the Cabinet Office, Historical and Records Section; the Commonwealth War Graves Commission; C.J. Coward; Miss A. Crawford; C.W. Daniel Co Ltd, Publishers; Elizabeth M. Davidson; Tony Froom; the General Register Office, Southport; I.D. Goode; The Earl Haig; R.D. Hanscombe; HMSO; the House of Commons, Library and Public Information Office; the House of Lords, Record Office; the Imperial War Museum, Departments of Documents, Printed Books, Photographs and Sound Records; D.J. Johnson; Kent Elms Library (all the staff); the Law Society; Major D.H. Lawrence; Peter Liddle BA MLitt PGCE FRHistS; Andrew Mackinlay MP; Ian Macmillan; the Rt Hon. John Major; the Ministry of Defence; the National Army Museum; the Newspaper Library, Colindale; News International plc; Kate O'Brien; Christopher Page; the Public Record Office; Julian Putkowski; Martin Rogers; Major P.K.R. Ross (retired); the Royal British Legion; the Royal Commission on Historical Manuscripts; the Royal Naval College, Greenwich; the Chief Naval Judge Advocate; Elaine Sellers; Mark Sellers; Neil Sellers; Miss Lisa Simmonds; Jonathan Spain; Bridget Spiers; Nigel Steel; *The Times*; The Right Hon. William Waldegrave PC MP; A.P. Watt Ltd; Mrs A. White.

I have not been able to trace the copyright holders of all the material I have quoted, and I would be pleased to hear from any whom I have not acknowledged.

For the loan of copyright photographs I am indebted to the following: The British Library, nos. 2 and 20; the Imperial War Museum, nos. 11, 12, 13, 14, 15 and 16; the Public Record Office, nos. 17 and 18; The Commonwealth War Graves Commission, no. 19.

Foreword

by Anthony Babington

The court-martial and execution of Sub-Lieutenant Dyett in 1916 has been referred to in several previous books, but this is the first book to be written entirely about the case.

Dyett's trial evoked a great deal of interest a few months after it had taken place. Horatio Bottomley, in a forthright article in *John Bull*, alleged that the young officer had been the victim of injustice, and the circumstances of the case were raised on more than one occasion in the House of Commons.

Interest was revived in 1919 when A. P. Herbert published his moving novel *The Secret Battle*, about an army officer who was shot at dawn after his unjust conviction by a court-martial in 1916. At the time of Dyett's trial both he and A. P. Herbert were serving in the Royal Naval Division, so it was generally assumed that *The Secret Battle* had been based on his case. The details of Dyett's trial were first revealed in 1983 in my own book *For the Sake of Example*, and were altogether different from the fictional trial depicted in A. P. Herbert's novel.

Leonard Sellers has performed a valuable task in collecting together all of the tragic circumstances of the Dyett case. He asks his readers, in the Introduction, to decide for themselves whether Dyett received justice. In formulating their decisions I would suggest that they should be careful to consider separately whether or not Dyett was guilty of the charge, and whether or not he should have been sentenced to death.

Dyett was charged with desertion, by failing to join his battalion in the line when it was his duty to do so. His defence was a simple one: although he had received orders to report to his battalion, he had been so confused by the state of chaos which existed near the front line, he had thought it sensible to return to his Brigade Headquarters for further orders. On the way back he lost his way, but the next day he reported to an officer from his Brigade called Lieutenant-Commander Egerton. It was obvious that Egerton would have been a crucial witness to substantiate this defence.

Dyett was defended by an officer called Trevanion who had qualified as a solicitor two years before the outbreak of war. He seems to have conducted the defence incredibly badly. For some unknown reason, in his cross-examination of the first prosecution witness, a Lieutenant-Commander, he elicited the damning facts that Dyett was a very poor officer, that he had a very nervous temperament, and that he considered himself to be unfit for the firing line. Trevanion followed this up by questioning a later witness about Dyett's demeanour at the moment he had turned back from the front line, and obtaining the answer that 'He looked as if he wanted to get out of it.'

By the time the prosecution case had finished, Trevanion had succeeded in little else but sowing the seeds for a verdict of 'guilty'. Dyett then informed the court that he neither wanted to give evidence himself nor to call any witnesses for the defence. Presumably he had made these two critical decisions on the advice of the Defending Officer – or certainly with his concurrence.

Up to this, the nature of the defence case had not been disclosed to the court. However, Trevanion had now availed himself of a little-used court-martial procedure whereby, in the closing address for the defence, statements could be made which were not supported by any evidence on oath, but which, if they were within the personal knowledge of the accused, had to be considered as being evidence nonetheless.

So the Court had heard from Trevanion's lips how Dyett

had made up his mind to return to Brigade Headquarters for further orders and how he had reported to Lieutenant-Commander Egerton. In this procedure neither Dyett nor Trevanion could be asked any questions about the defence case.

If Dyett had told his story on oath and had been able to call any evidence to support his contention that he had reported back to a superior officer, the outcome of the trial might well have been different.

Horatio Bottomley alleged that Dyett had not seen his Defending Officer until half-an-hour before the trial had commenced. If this was true, it was a grave injustice. On the other hand, the Prosecution asserted that there had been a four-hour conference between Dyett and Trevanion the day before the trial. In the circumstance of the case, this should have been more than adequate. In my own experience as a defending officer during the Second World War, and as a defence counsel in the post-war years, an interview lasting for an hour or two with the accused was generally sufficient if the facts of the case were simple.

Some suggestion has been made that Dyett's trial was legally flawed because no Summary of Evidence was taken beforehand. I do not regard the absence of a Summary in Dyett's court-martial file as in any way sinister. During the early 1980s the Ministry of Defence granted me privileged access to the court-martial files of all the 346 officers and men of the British Army who had been condemned to death and executed during the First World War. These files were, at that time, closed to public inspection. Not one of the files included a Summary of Evidence. I feel certain that Capt. Griffith-Jones, the Judge Advocate at Dyett's court-martial, who was an experienced barrister, would not have allowed the trial to proceed if there had been anything amiss with the legal procedure.

Introduction

During research for my book on the history of the Hood Battalion of the Royal Naval Division (*The Hood Battalion*, Leo Cooper, 1995) I came across reference to the court martial and execution of a Temporary Sub-Lieutenant of the Nelson Battalion, RND. The story held my attention and began to fascinate and disturb me. Was this young man of just 21 years guilty of the offence charged? And did he deserve to be executed by firing party on a cold January dawn? Did he receive justice or was he a pawn in the maintenance of good order and military discipline during the First World War?

My concern and apprehension grew as I delved deeper into the records and the story unfolded. I have tried to show both sides of the argument. It is for you, the reader, to make a judgment: your background and personality will have a bearing on the conclusion you reach. All I ask, whichever side you come down on, is that you at least have sympathy for his memory. He was after all a volunteer, not a professional soldier, who had weaknesses, like the best of us. The greatest hero who has ever lived had his Achilles' heel. Try to place yourself back in the early days of the century. How would you have fared?

To wait throughout the night for death at the hands of your comrades, not for murder or any crime punishable in civilian life, must have been an ordeal of genuine horror. This was the fate of some 307 men during the war. At the end of the story ask yourself the questions: did Dyett receive justice? and should a full review of the files of the execution be undertaken? But also ask yourself one additional question: Could you have fired the shot? I ask no more.

Leonard Sellers
Honeysuckle House
Eastwood

CHAPTER ONE

Dispatch of Death

Thomas MacMillan, a clerk at 189th Brigade HQ of the Royal Naval Division writes:

I had not been many days in my job when I was faced with a most unpleasant duty.

There was nothing to attract me outside the office and I was alone one evening at a late hour when I heard a dispatch rider drawing up in the courtyard. He left his engine panting and handed me the letter he was commissioned to carry, at the time remarking that he had to wait for an acknowledgment.

I opened the envelope and was shocked to find an order from Division to put to death at dawn a young officer who had been tried by General Court Martial for cowardice in the face of the enemy.

I instructed the dispatch rider to stand by, and hurried to the mess. The officers had long since finished their dinner and were diverting themselves before a roaring fire when I entered.

From my grave demeanour the Major guessed that something serious was afoot and, taking the communication, he read it aloud. To make doubly certain, he read the message a second time with great deliberation. In answer to his query, I told him that the dispatch rider was waiting further orders.

I was dismissed and shortly afterwards the Major

appeared with instructions for the execution of the dastardly deed, which he handed personally to the dispatch rider for delivery.

The night was spoiled for me, for this was the first case to my knowledge of a man in our Division being done to death in the name of good order and military discipline and an officer at that![1]

So what was the story of this unfortunate officer, the only member of the Royal Naval Division, and one of only three officers, to be executed, during the First World War? Decades of supposition, conjecture, questions in the House of Commons, articles, books and misinformation have been debated, circulated and argued over. Now, with the evidence of the court-martial file, I am able to place on record what took place at the hearing concerning Dyett's actions at the Battle of the Ancre, on 13/14 November, 1916, and the following days. For this young man a chain of events led to his execution by his comrades.

The Royal Naval Division, consisting of two Brigades of naval reservists and one Brigade of Marines, had been formed in August, 1914, by the Admiralty, under the guiding hand of Winston Churchill, The First Lord, and administered by the Board. At this early stage of the war Britain had a serious shortfall in infantry divisions. The Navy, on the other hand, had a large number of reservists over and above those required for manning the fleet. The ideal solution appeared to be the formation of a Royal Naval Division, still under the control of the Admiralty, but fighting as infantry. So men of the Royal Naval Reserve, stokers of the Royal Fleet Reserve and officers and men of the Royal Naval Volunteer Reserve, supplemented later by men from the six recruiting areas of London, Bristol, Liverpool, Sussex, Clyde, and Tyne and Wear were called to the colours.

The naval battalions were named after famous Admirals and were constituted as follows:

1st Royal Naval Brigade	1st Battalion (Drake)
	2nd Battalion (Hawke)
	3rd Battalion (Benbow)
	4th Battalion (Collingwood)
2nd Royal Naval Brigade	5th Battalion (Nelson)
	6th Battalion (Howe)
	7th Battalion (Hood)
	8th Battalion (Anson)
3rd Royal Naval Brigade (Marines)	9th Battalion (Portsmouth)
	10th Battalion (Plymouth)
	11th Battalion (Chatham)
	12th Battalion (Deal)

Back in those early days of the war in 1914 and early 1915 idealism and a sense of liberation and adventure drove the hearts and minds of many of the new volunteer officers and men. They have been called the Tipperary Days by a Chaplain of the 2nd Brigade.[2] Poets, musicians, composers, writers and sportsmen had answered the call to arms. The flower of British and Dominion youth had rallied in the name of patriotism and wonder at the larger-than-life events unfolding before their eyes. Few wished to miss out on the fleeting experience. For fleeting it would be – the war would soon be won. Justice and right would prevail. People like Rupert Brooke, Bernard Freyberg, Septimus 'Cleg' Kelly, Patrick Shaw-Stewart, Arthur Asquith, Denis Browne, A.P. Herbert and Compton Mackenzie joined the colours. A number of them were friends of Winston Churchill and his private secretary, Edward Marsh. Oxbridge and the public schools gave of their best.

However, the old guard – the stokers and reservists who had served before the war – hated the idea of soldiering and wanted to be back in the Navy. As Patrick Shaw-Stewart was to write of the stokers in January, 1915:

They have got a sort of standing grievance in the back of their evil old minds that they want to be back in their steel-walled pen, yelping delight and rolling in the waist, instead of forming fours under the orders of an insolent young landlubber.[3]

The stokers were often men over 30 years of age and would prove to be excellent fighters and the early backbone of the Division. The original Naval Volunteer officers also yearned for the sea, and showed it as, when the news broke that their destiny was to be infantry, some took part in a mock ceremony, lowering the Admiralty Seamanship Manual into the waves.

A large number of the commanding officers were from the Guards, charged with welding this diverse collection of ex-seamen and an enthusiastic assortment of men from miners to poets into disciplined, effective infantry. It was not going to be easy.

However, there were a number of factors in the Division's favour. Major-General Sir Archibald Paris was appointed to its command and he soon came to appreciate the quality of the men he commanded. A great affection grew between him and his officers, and the rank and file, as he guided and led them between 1914 and 1916 until he was seriously injured by artillery fire in France in October, 1916.

The Division did not have to heed the views of the War Office too closely, since its officers included Arthur Asquith, the Prime Minister's son, and (as mentioned) friends of the First Lord and his private secretary; it was Admiralty-run and had easy access to the ear of government and power.

The Division was sent to Walmer, but shortly afterwards the 2nd Brigade transferred to Lord Northbourne's land at Betteshanger. But in October, 1914, before the Battalions had time to jell as infantry, the call came for action. They were dispatched to Europe to defend the Belgian fortress of Antwerp, a further line of defence of our gateways to Europe, the Channel Ports. Without artillery support, the situation became hopeless and the Royal Naval Division had to withdraw. Battle continued while troops and countless civilians were evacuated, but orders became confused and, due to mistakes and lack of communication, much of the 1st Brigade was interned in Holland.

By November, 1914, a new training camp had been completed at Blandford in Dorset, and the Battalions moved there in stages from various locations around England. In the meantime a training establishment had been opened at Crystal Palace, in which the Great Exhibition had been held in the previous century. In the courts and halls, green recruits, officers and specialists were knocked into shape before being transferred to Blandford for a final polish.

H.V. Clark, a seaman at Crystal Palace, wrote a small booklet called *Observations on the Life and Characters at the Crystal Palace*. One example of his work is a poem called: 'Parody on The Rajah of Bhong' and is set out below to give the reader a flavour of the times:

> We've cut off our curls, said 'Good-bye' to the girls.
> And embraced the calling nautical;
> To the Palace we've come, and we're making things hum,
> Tho' often we're found in a pickle.
> And I'm sure you'll agree when our good ship you see,
> She's as smart and as safe as a liner;
> While her men slick and trim, full of vigour and vim,
> Are 'some' sailors – there aren't any finer!

> (Chorus)

> Peace!, Peace!, we'll all welcome Peace,
> I think all this warfare is wrong;
> For I hate PTI and I oft sit and sigh,
> For the beautiful valley of Bhong!

> Now we're caught in the fold, and do as we're told,
> And our 'Won'ts' – well – we have to suppress them;
> And if orders aren't clear, and we cannot quite hear,
> Our instructors expect us to guess them.
> We take scoldings and snubs from juvenile 'subs.',
> Who address us with due condescension.

We drill and we 'grub', we guard and we scrub,
Our tasks are too varied to mention.

(Chorus)

Peace!, Peace!, we'll all welcome Peace,
We think early rising is wrong;
For we never Parade, and we're always well paid.
In the beautiful valley of Bhong!

Altho' we've to work, and it's treason to shirk.
Yet life here has much compensation.
We've 'pictures' and games, and concerts and 'flames'.
Our Revue proved a mighty sensation.
It's called 'Form two deep!', and you laugh, till you weep,
At the antics of Boen, Howell and 'Clappy',
While 'the Beauties in line' made the Chorus so fine,
No wonder the 'Ratings' looked happy!

(Chorus)

Peace!, Peace!, we'll all welcome Peace
And bury our troubles in song,
And we will not forget the artistes, you bet,
There's a stage for them always at Bhong![4]

Rumour began to circulate that the Division was to take part in the Dardanelles campaign. Rupert Brooke was to write: 'The best expedition of the war. Figure me celebrating the first Holy Mass in St Sophia since 1453'.[5]

On 25 February, 1915, the King and Winston Churchill inspected the Division at a place called Three Mile Point, near the grounds of the present Blandford camp. As Violet Asquith reported, Churchill was glowing with pride in his troops. On the 27th and 28th the expedition left Avonmouth for the east and the adventure had begun. The peninsula of Gallipoli was where the hard work of training would be put to the test.

Between 25 April, when the Division took part in a

diversionary exercise in the Gulf of Saros, and battled and bled at Anzac and Helles, and the evacuation on 9 January, 1916, the RND had changed out of all recognition. The fresh, young, eager and intelligent had been killed, maimed or disillusioned. The flower of the generation had gone. Harder, grinding, relentless times were coming. Soaring minds and hopes could not influence artillery.

Licking their wounds, assessing and reforming on the nearby islands of Lemnos, Imbros and Tenedos, a policing role beckoned. Break-up and disbandment was rumoured and put into motion. An extensive rearguard action was fought to save it. Vice Admiral De Robeck telegraphed the Admiralty: 'The men, who have fought magnificently, have great esprit de corps and the units are up to war strength.'[6]

In London the Division's influence was being felt in high places as lobbying began. Still it was a slow process and the break-up started. Major-General Paris, with heavy heart, left for a holiday, convinced that his proud Division's life was at an end. Still matters were progressing between the War Office and the Admiralty. A compromise was reached in that the Division would be transferred to the War Office and placed under the Army Act[7] and the Commander-in-Chief of the British Armies in France. A complete transfer could not be agreed due to the legal status of the officers and men, and the Admiralty remained paymaster.

By May, 1916, the Division was in France, bearing the title 63rd (RN) Division. Army battalions had been allocated to bolster its numbers. Artillery was added, with the full supporting units that made up a British fighting Division.

188th Brigade
(Brigadier-General H.E.S. Prentice DSO)
Howe Battalion
Anson Battalion
1st RMLI Battalion
2nd RMLI Battalion

189th Brigade
(Brigadier-General Lewis Francis Phillips DSO)
Hood Battalion
Hawke Battalion
Drake Battalion
Nelson Battalion

190th Brigade
(Brigadier-General Trotman CB)
1st Battalion Honourable Artillery Company
4th Bedford Battalion
7th Royal Fusiliers
10th Dublin Fusiliers

The Division needed to be retrained. Their battle experience in France would be entirely different from Gallipoli. On the peninsula there was a shortfall in artillery, trenches were only a matter of yards apart and hand-to-hand fighting and constant vigilance were required. On the Western Front artillery was master, sending torrents of shell and shrapnel towards you. Fate hung not on your ability, man for man, but on lady luck and random selection, in a mutilating hell. The front line was manned only by small advanced parties.

When Major-General Paris became a victim of the barrage, the War Office decided that this unconforming excrescence of a Division needed bringing into line and standardizing to the army model. Nothing was more irritating to the Sandhurst mind than this extravagant and illogical upholding of naval tradition. The land was not for sailors.

The RND regarded nautical parlance as the backbone of its separate identity. It was not about to relinquish its traditions without a fight. Its camps were run on naval lines. A ship's bell kept watches, leaving camp was to go ashore and being late in returning was being adrift. The White Ensign flew and one was allowed to grow a beard. The other ranks included Petty Officers and Leading Seamen; officers could be Commanders or Commodores.

The War Office's answer as replacement was one Major-

General Cameron Deane Shute, via the Welsh Regiment and Rifle Brigade. He was the man chosen to knock them into shape. He took up his post with a deep apprehension and crusading spirit that upset all ranks. Indeed, A.P. Herbert was to write a poem, the first line of which reads: 'The General inspecting the trenches', and made mention of – 'that shit Shute'.[8] The General's views would later change to grudging admiration.

Edwin Leopold Arthur Dyett was born on 7 October, 1895, in Albany Road, Roath, Cardiff. His father was Walter Henry Ross Dyett,[9] later in the First World War to be Chief Naval Transport Officer at Liverpool Naval Base. His mother was Mary Constance Dyett, formerly Bird. His family had extensive military connections. Commander Dyett was a distant cousin of General Sir John French, the Commander-in-Chief of the British Expeditionary Force. On his mother's side, a Surgeon Bird took part in the Siege of Lucknow during the Indian Mutiny. Both his grandfathers held the rank of colonel and later became Military Knights of Windsor.[10]

Edwin Dyett was commissioned on 24 June, 1915, at the Crystal Palace Depot, and was transferred to Blandford camp on 16 October of that year. On 16 February, 1916, he embarked to join his Battalion on the Greek islands, after their evacuation from the Gallipoli Peninsula, later to disembark at Marseilles on 22 May, 1916, when the Division was ordered to France.[11]

He volunteered for service wide-eyed and expectant, but the path to his personal Armageddon was set – in just 20 months he would be shot at dawn by his brothers in arms.

References

1. Imperial War Museum, Department of Documents: Thomas MacMillan.

2. Foster, The Rev. H.C., 'Antwerp Adventure: Shells and Burning Oil', p. 185, from *The Great War: I Was There*, Amalgamated Press, 1939.

3. Knox, Ronald, *Patrick Shaw-Stewart*, Collins, 1920, p. 110.

4. Clark, H.V., *Observations on the Life and Characters at the Crystal Palace* (unpublished).

5. Keyes, Sir Geoffrey, *The Letters of Rupert Brooke*, Faber, 1968: letter to Dudley Ward of 20 February 1915, p. 660.

6. Public Record Office, Kew, ref. ADM/116/1411.

7. Public Record Office, Kew, ref. ADM/137/3084. Note: on the islands after Gallipoli, Lieut.-Col. E.J. Stroud began a series of lectures on Military Law to members of the RND.

8. Bentham, John Henry – taken from *A Young Officer's Diary* at the Liddle Collection, University of Leeds. This poem was found in his papers and is by A.P. Herbert.

9. General Register Office, certified copy of an entry of birth, application number G 004879, ref. WBXZ 014158.

10. *The Times*, Saturday, 20 August, 1983.

11. MOD, Whitehall Library, Royal Naval Division Books ROS 182 & 183: Officer's Service, 1914–1919, Vols 1 & 2.

CHAPTER TWO

The Nelson at the Ancre

In a world war there is an event, a conflict or battle that changes the whole ethos of a nation. Such a moment was 1 July, 1916, the first day of the Battle of the Somme. From that time on everything was different. Now the telegrams of death were all too often the harbingers for lost and destroyed communities. Be the men regular, territorial or of the New Army, the reaper had no favourites.

The battle had ebbed and flowed and progress had been slow, but by October the high ground of Thiepval Ridge was in the hands of the British. However, the situation was not nearly so satisfactory to the north, on both sides of the River Ancre, a tributary of the Somme. The Germans remained fixed and unyielding on both sides of this river, at Grandcourt and across the river at Beaucourt-sur-Ancre and up to Beaumont Hamel and Serre. This resulted in a clearly defined salient that the British urgently needed to take. A number of factors applied. The French were demanding a final flourish by their allies, before winter set in so as to support their own efforts at Verdun. General Gough of the Fifth Army was to have this task and Sir Douglas Haig, the Commander-in-Chief, had given him a free hand. It was to be his decision as to whether it was possible to attack before winter held fast the ground, their hopes and their aspirations. He would look for any window of opportunity the weather allowed. Haig needed to mollify the French in their demands for British aggression. As events unfolded he would be able to attend the Chantilly

Conference armed with the blessing of a British success in battle still fresh in his mind. This would tip the balance in Britain's favour – a balance seldom kept level by such unequal partners.

Sir Douglas Haig had seen General Gough at Toutencourt on Sunday, 12 November, and wrote in his diary:

> Had been round all the Divisions and most of the Brigades detailed for the attack. Their commanders all now thought that we had a fair chance of success. He himself [Gough] recommended that the attack should go in. I told him that a success at this time was much wanted, first on account of the situation in Rumania. It is important that we should prevent the enemy from withdrawing any Divisions from France to that theatre. Next the feeling in Russia is not favourable either to the French or ourselves. We are thought to be accomplishing little. The Germans' party in Russia spreads these reports. Lastly, on account of the Chantilly Conference which meets on Wednesday. The British position will doubtless be much stronger (as memories are short) if I could appear there on the top of the capture of Beaumont Hamel for instance, and 300 German prisoners. It would show too that we had no intention of ceasing to press the enemy on the Somme. But the necessity for a success must not blind our eyes to the difficulties of ground and weather. Nothing is so costly as a failure! But I am ready to run reasonable risks.[1]

On 3 May, 1916, the Headquarters of the Division produced a nominal roll of officers then serving in each Battalion. The Nelson Battalion's roll is as follows:

NOMINAL ROLL OF OFFICERS, NELSON BATTALION, RND

Substantive Rank	Temp Rank	Name	Regiment	Appointment
Major	Lieut.-Col.	N.O. Burge	RMLI	OC

	Lt-Cdr	E.W. Nelson	RNVR
	Lieut.	H.T. Ely	RNVR
Lieutenant		J.A. Gates	RMLI
	A/Lieuts	G.K. Turnbull	RNVR
		C.S. Hosking	
	Lieut.	C. Truscott	
	Sub-Lieuts	B. Dangerfield	
		B. Batchelor	
		E.L.A. Dyett	
		H.R. Pearson	
		E.J.B. Lloyd	
		A.L. Ball	
		W.D. Redmond	
		J. Cowans	
		F.E. Rees	
		E.W. Squires	
		S. Flowitt	
		W.D. Walker	
		A.P. Mecklenburg	
		A.P. Taylor	
		J.E. Greenwell	
		H.V.S. Johnson	
		L.S. Gardner	
		H.S. Strickland	
		J.H. Emerson	
Surgeon	Sub-Lieut	A.B. Parker	RN
	Lt-Cdr	H.R. Robson	RNVR
	Sub-Lieuts	D. Francis	
		A.K. Smithells	
		D. Galloway[2]	

From this listing we see that Edwin Dyett was in France with his Battalion in May. By the time of the Battle of the Ancre other officers had come and gone from the Nelson. The Commanding Officer was Lieutenant-Colonel N.O. Burge who had served as a Captain of Marines in the cruiser *Berwick*. He was with the Royal Naval Division at Antwerp in October, 1914, as Major Burge, with the Portsmouth Battalion, acting as Temporary Adjutant. Later, at Gallipoli, he was in command of the Royal Marine Cyclists' Company. In July, 1915, he assumed command of the Nelson Battalion, 1st Naval Brigade. However, he was to be invalided from the peninsula in October, but returned to command the RND's rendezvous point during the evacuation. This was near Morto Bay and was a very responsible position. The Battalion was therefore well served by having such an experienced officer in command.[3]

The 63rd (RN) Division was now to be blooded in a major action, having completed its training in the ways of the army. Due to its lack of experience in France in any large offensive operations, General Shute held two conferences for Brigadiers, Brigade Staffs and all his Commanding Officers. During these preparations it was found that new trenches would have to be constructed to facilitate the forming-up of the troops prior to the attack.[4] This extra work put an additional strain on the troops, but was to prove sensible and far-sighted.

The Nelson's Battalion Order Number 50 of 25 October, 1916, outlines the planning as follows: the 189th Infantry Brigade was to take part in the attack on enemy positions situated on the north of the River Ancre. The date of the attack would be known as Z day. The Brigade was to attack with two battalions in the front line and with two following. The Hood was to be on the right, alongside the river, with the Hawke on their left. The Drake was to be in the rear of the Hood and the Nelson in the rear of the Hawke. To the left, northwards, was to be the 188th Infantry Brigade, with the Howe next to the Hawke and the Anson alongside the Nelson.

In the plan of attack the Nelson was to be formed up in four waves immediately in the rear of the Hawke, under and close up to the bank behind Roberts Trench, with its left flank resting on Louvercy Street Trench. Each wave was to consist of four platoons, one from each Company, and was to be formed from right to left as follows – A Company, C, D, and then B. The waves were to follow each other at a distance of ten yards between the first and second waves and forty yards between the second and third and also the fourth. The leading wave of the Nelson had to follow the fourth wave of the Hawke at a distance of 150 yards. It was noted that the initial obstacles in front of the Nelson (and not in front of the Hawke) necessitated that the Nelson should move off as fast as possible after the leading battalion. The intervals between waves could be corrected after they had passed their objective of the front-line trench.

The plan was that the Hood and Hawke should capture the first objective, the German Front-Line Reserve Trench (marked on the plan as the dotted green line) and would then clean up all three enemy lines. It was hoped that this objective would be captured at 0018 hours. Then, at 0023 hours the second objective should be obtained when the Drake and Nelson Battalions were to pass through the Hood and Hawke and move on to capture the green line. The first and second waves were to advance straight through to this line and were to reorganize at once. The third wave should clear up the dug-outs in Station Road and the fourth wave should clear up the dotted blue line and the numerous dug-outs on the reserve slope of the hill.

There was then to be a halt of about 30 minutes on the green line, during which there would be two pauses of 5 minutes in the 18 pounders' barrage. At the end of the second pause an intense barrage would reopen and the Hood and Hawke would pass through the Drake and Nelson and capture the yellow line. They would then wait for 30 minutes on this line to allow the Drake and Nelson to close up to within 150 yards of the two advanced Battalions.[5] The object of all this planning was the capture of the village of Beaucourt-sur-Ancre. Events were to prove that matters seldom go according to plan, but there would be much bravery and the village would fall to the RND.

This order was followed up on 27 October by the Adjutant of the Nelson with order number 51. This dealt with the administrative arrangements for the attack. It was hoped that one field kitchen per battalion would be got up as far as Hamel, and it was arranged that only five cooks from the Nelson would be required, two of whom would be with a forward kitchen. All surplus gear not accompanying the battalion was to be dumped in an unoccupied billet in Englebelmer, in the barn adjoining the Town Mayor's Office, billet number 104. The report also covered such matters as casualties, SOS, prisoners, petrol tins, pre-servation of supplies, nominal rolls, documents, surplus officers, ammunition, rations and carrying parties.[6]

Now all that was required was a change in the weather. Joseph Murray, a seaman in the Hood Battalion, gives his account before the battle:

On the 12th, the day before the Battle of the Ancre, we were in Menil. Sub-Lieutenant Hart came round and said, 'Come on lads, hurry up, we have got to leave as soon as we can after lunch, its on.' That's all, we knew what he meant. Well it was 2 o'clock when we left. So we got to Hamel, the village a bit nearer the firing line, by platoons at a time, that's fifteen men, near enough.

The Quartermaster decided to get rid of some of his surplus rations. First of all we were issued with two bombs, two P bombs, phosphorous bombs, new things to us, we hadn't seen them before. They were a little bit longer, but like a jam tin. And we had a couple of Mills bombs; this was the first time I had seen Mills bombs to handle. All the rest had been artificial. The whole point was to make sure that the pin was in. Also we got two sacks of bombs per section.

Bless my heart and soul if they didn't come round with the rations. We were given a tin of jam each! Now we never had one each the whole time that we were in the army. And most of us were also dished out with a glass jar of Piccadilly [picalilli]! Never seen the damn stuff before!

Well, we had got to get out of Hamel and were dressed up like a Father Christmas. You know, we had hanging here a mug, hanging there a cap. And an entrenching tool at the back beating out a tattoo on your backside. And you had a haversack and a sack of bombs round your neck and so on. Like a blinking Christmas Tree.

Anyhow we had to get out of Hamel, because the people we had left at Menil had to move forward. We were the front-line attacking troops. So we were ahead of everybody, every time, all the time. We got outside of Hamel and it was still daylight, being round about 5 o'clock. Now we couldn't get forward because of the daylight and because there were observation barrage balloons, and there were planes flying across the sky. (During the period at Menil we saw a number of planes come down. I think there were 2 or 3 of ours and about 4 of theirs altogether. One of ours fell quite near us, and he was burnt to death.) We hid in the disused trenches outside Hamel. A colleague said 'Look Lucky I'm not carrying this bastard stuff any longer.' So we opened the tin of jam and ate it. We said, 'We very rarely get treated to a tin of jam and we must not upset the Quartermaster by throwing it away.' And we eat the Pickle Lilly! Well the Pickle Lilly didn't agree with the jam or the jam didn't agree with the Pickle Lilly I don't know, but I know the results afterwards![7]

When it was dark the Battalions moved forward across the open ground following a white tape up to the firing line. Each battalion formed up in four distinct waves, until some twelve lines of men were lying out in the open. It was very damp and a thick mist hung in the air. As hour followed hour, men attempted to sleep. Good luck messages were passed around. Colonel Freyberg of the Hood, on the rounds of his Battalion, stated that most of the men seemed to be in another world. He was to ask his troops the next day what they had been thinking about and they all replied that their thoughts were of the future, none thinking of the past.[8]

J.Hall of the Royal Naval Division's Medical Unit gives his account:

I can recall the lads with their black faces, with their bayonets and ammunition in front and bombs and that sort of thing. I remember passing along there and seeing their faces, I still feel and felt for them, going over the top.[9]

At 5.15 am there was a stirring all along the line. Greatcoats were removed and, contrary to all warnings, the slight sound of the wooden entrenching tool handle against the bayonet scabbard could be heard. Tea was brewed, for many to be their last. The hands of the clock were moving inexorably towards Z hour. Aeroplanes should have co-operated in the attack, with flares; unfortunately the fog made this impossible.[10]

The intense barrage opened as the signal for the advance. But, owing to the mist, the last wave of the Hawke Battalion, which should have been seen just 150 yards ahead of the Nelson's first wave, was lost from view. The German barrage was negligible but heavy machine-gun fire opened up on the Nelson about the time that their fourth wave crossed their original front line. The Battalion suffered a considerable number of casualties, unfortunately losing a high percentage of officers.[11] The 189th Infantry Brigade report of the action was to state:

> Nelson Battalion advanced close up to the barrage and suffered considerably from our own artillery fire. Still the first two lines advanced and, keeping in touch with the barrage, arrived at the steep bank, situated between the German 3rd line and Station Road, known as the Terraces. They met considerable opposition, but, after hand-to-hand fighting with bombs and the bayonet, the remainder advanced to Station Road. Dugouts here were cleared with little opposition and the advance continued to the green line with difficulty.
>
> Meanwhile the 3rd and 4th waves encountered very heavy sustained enfilading machine-gun fire and suffered very heavy casualties and lost cohesion and direction and, except for small detached parties, ceased to exist as a fighting force. Battalion HQ passed the original front line at about 6.30am and advanced into no-man's-land, but then came under very heavy fire itself, from close range. It afterwards transpired that a proportion of the German front-line system was still holding out in a stronghold. In front of this the Nelson's

Commanding Officer and Adjutant were both killed. This strong point was holding up a large number of troops from all battalions by its heavy machine-gun fire. Therefore the RND men began to dig in and at this time Lieutenant Dangerfield, the Nelson's Signal Officer, did excellent work in rallying parties of men who had lost their officers, in an endeavour to organize an attack against the strong point. He also ran a line out to the HQ of his Battalion, although slightly wounded in the hand.[12]

J.E. Frazer, an AB with the Hawke Battalion, describes the battle as follows:

My position was in the fourth wave and was in a position so as to see when the bombardment first started at 6 o'clock in the morning. The effect of the shelling was that the German front line appeared as if it was filled or being filled with molten metal. There was a glare in the sky and it was against that glare that we were able to see the first wave who had been lying just clear of the very broad broken belt of barbed wire that had been broken up previously by artillery and toffee apples. The idea was that men could move through.

When the time came, it was my turn to go over the top. Our NCO, Petty Officer McDonald of the signals section, climbed up on to the original no-man's-land and turned round and faced us, conducting like an orchestra, and said, 'Come on boys, this is war!' And he led us across no-man's-land. But we hadn't got very far when the Germans turned their machine guns on us. My first feeling was that someone had lost their bearings and turned the guns on us. See, there was three waves of men already in advance of us and a tremendous bombardment. I couldn't understand how there could be anybody left.

Anyhow we eventually arrived in this very broad belt of barbed wire and the machine guns turned on us again. Of course it was November and very misty. The sparks that were shining were coming out as the bullets were hitting the wire, they were like diamonds. We stood for a moment or two and wondered what had happened. Then we got down into one of the shell holes that had been made by the toffee apples. We kept looking out to see if there were any officers moving forward, that we could move forward with. It was just at that time that I noticed our Commanding Officer, Leslie Wilson. He was standing up firing his revolver and we couldn't see who he was firing at. He was closer to the Germans than us.

The next impression I got was when things quietened down. One of our men was up against the barbed wire with a very bad wound. And Petty Officer McDonald got out of the shell hole and was going to render assistance to this man. And one single shot went out and old McDonald was then on his fours. Eventually a sniper had got him, you see. And he turned round and, with his head down like a real old soldier, went down into the hole, which he had just left. As his legs came down into the hole, they turned the machine gun on him. And you could see his trousers getting blown away! They were taking the legs off him![13]

In the meantime a body of troops, about 100 strong, that had got through to the green line continued to advance when the barrage lifted and occupied a position in the yellow line. Here they found that they were not in touch on either flank. After a report had been received that troops were holding the yellow line just west of Beaucourt, this party of Nelson moved after dusk to a position on the left and in touch with them. From that moment the Nelson had ceased to exist as a separate identity, as losses had been far too heavy.[14]

W.E. Bland, an AB of the Nelson Battalion, gives his account:

Our second in command, who was there, had the good

fortune to say, 'I think you will find the safest way is up by the railway.' The road and the river ran parallel at that point. Because on the other side was a redoubt which was holding out and it turned out afterwards that it accounted for one of our sections, completely wiped them out. We made our way and we came to what I think was known as the yellow line, which was our objective, and established our guns. Our men were all dead tired, so tired that they were falling asleep. And all the time we were anticipating a counter-attack by the Germans from Beaumont Hamel, which fortunately never developed.

Shortly after that, I cannot remember why, I was sent off to find the Brigade Major for further instructions. And it was whilst I was on the road that a high explosive came over and hit the road close by, which put an end to my active service. [A fragment of the shell hit Bland's right cheekbone. The concussion of the shell destroyed the nerves in his eye, but the eye was not actually touched.]

A terrific trumpeting went on in my head. And I thought to myself, is this being killed? I remember very little until my Petty Officer, Wallace Denleigh, said, 'Come on, I will help you to the Dressing Station'. I had got various wounds. I had a fractured clavicle and numerous flesh wounds, on the right hand side of the body. These were attended to and then I was put on a stretcher and carried by four German prisoners down the line to a waiting ambulance. [Subsequently, when the Royal Naval Division memorial was put up outside Beaumont to commemorate its part in the action, according to the Petty Officer Denleigh, the site chosen was, by chance, the precise location where he found Bland injured and in need of attention.][15]

J. Hall, of the Royal Naval Division's Medical Unit, continues:

I remember bringing a man out and we were trudging

with this fellow over shell holes when we heard this shell coming. Well I had been long enough out there and on Gallipoli to know when a shell was coming near. So we stopped and we just waited for it, you see. And the damned thing landed 3 or 4 yards away and never exploded. It fell among the bricks and mud and so on, knocked the helmet off one of my pals and showered the dirt all over us, and we had this fellow on top of a stretcher.[16]

Thomas MacMillan, a clerk with the 189th Brigade HQ, wrote:

As officer after officer 'went under', the non-commissioned officers left standing carried on in a manner beyond all praise. I instance the case of Petty Officer Wilson of the Nelson Battalion who, after his officer had been laid low, led what remained of his platoon forward to its objective and, observing his Battalion Commander fall before the redoubt, advanced against this strong point and fought till not a soul remained alive.[17]

Sub-Lieutenant R.B. Rackham (later a Brigadier) of the Hawke Battalion takes up the account:

It was a terrible day for the Hawke Battalion which in the early stages was devastated. I should say within 20 minutes of the opening of the battle the Hawke Battalion as a fighting force almost ceased to exist.

I didn't go over in the first line; I came over in a later line and there was a German strong point, which had not been dealt with by the gunners or the leading troops. And one could see the Germans there. Actually I saw one shooting at me, and I dropped down and unfortunately my batman, behind me, caught it, falling on me and died on me, as a result. We couldn't do much all that day but the following day two tanks were sent up and by various manoeuvres (I think that the Germans were so frightened by the tanks) they simply surrendered and this strong point was mopped up. But it had done amazing damage against the battalions that had come up against it.

It was very elaborate. The machine guns were on lifts, down in the dug-out and were simply lifted up and came into position on top. I would think there were half a dozen machine guns in that strong point, an area of about a circular 100 yards. The Ancre area slopes down quite steeply and then up the other side to Thiepval. We were just on the level, as it were, and that is where this strong point was and devastated both the Hawke and Nelson Battalions. It didn't rise up above ground level. The machine guns came up, with its crew mounted on these lifts by manual means, a winding handle used by people below. As a result the Battalion on the top were very badly mauled. But those on the slope and down to the river, mainly the Hood and Hawke, were most successful. The strong point didn't really cover that area for two reasons, one because they were shielded from it, and secondly because of the amazing leadership given to the Hood by Colonel Freyberg, which resulted in his VC.

During the night, what were called our first re-inforcements, which were left behind, came up and joined us. So we had other officers, among whom was the Assistant Adjutant, one A.P. Herbert. He came and joined me with our little band, I think we had only 30 to 40 men left. [Rackham was to be hit in the hand and was, he thinks, about the only surviving officer of his Battalion.][18]

By 3pm Colonel Freyberg of the Hood Battalion had assumed command of all the remaining troops and had reported that he was in touch with the Cambridgeshire Regiment on the right, on the other side of the river. He was also in touch with about 150 men of the 188th Brigade on the left. Good communications with the Brigade were maintained throughout the operations, by telephone and by runners, who brought in sketches of the positions and frequent reports. Freyberg asked that the barrage be raised further forward to enable him to take the crest of the hill to the east of Beaucourt as he was suffering numerous casualties from snipers while consolidating the line. Battle patrols had been pushed out towards the village but had to return owing to casualties from their own barrage.

The situation by 8pm was that 250 Hoods, 115 Drakes, 15 Nelsons and some 50 men of the 188th Brigade, most of whom belonged to the Anson, were consolidating on the green line. Additionally three Companies of the HAC, about 360 strong, were in support. Brigade Headquarters could obtain no communication with the Nelson or Hawke Battalions; runners were sent with messages and orders but did not return.

During the night the Brigade was reinforced by one battalion from the 111th Brigade, the 13th King's Royal Rifle Corps, who came up on the left in the yellow line. At 5.15am on the 14th orders were received that an attack was going to be made from the green line at 6am to bring the left level with the Brigade. At 7.45am Freyberg led an attack on the village of Beaucourt. In spite of heavy machine-gun and rifle fire to start with, the attack was completely successful and a very large number of prisoners were taken. Freyberg was badly injured, but for his efforts was to be awarded the VC.[19]

The Nelson Battalion suffered the following Casualties.

Officers killed

Lieutenant-Colonel	N.O. Burge
Sub-Lieutenants	J.H. Emerson
	E.W. Cashmore
	A.L. Ball
	L.S. Gardner
	D. Francis
	E.W. Squires
	E. Langstreth
	D.R.G.P. Alldridge
	G.A. Reddick

Officers wounded

Lieutenant-Commander	D. Galloway
Lieutenants	B. Dangerfield [remained on duty]
Lieutenants	S. Flowitt
Sub-Lieutenants	E.J.B. Lloyd
	A.K. Smithells
	A.P. Mecklenburg
	J.R. Savacy
	F.W. Ghardin
	E.V.G. Gardner [remained on duty]

Other ranks

Killed	24
Wounded	195
Missing	120
Gassed	1

A number of congratulatory messages was received by the Brigade:

From HM the King to Sir Douglas Haig
I heartily congratulate you on the great success achieved by my gallant troops during the last three days in the advance on both sides of the Ancre. This further capture of the enemy's front-line trenches under special difficulties owing to the recent wet weather redounds to the credit of all ranks.

From Commander-in-Chief to GOC, Fifth Army
The Commander-in-Chief warmly congratulates you and your troops on the great result of your operations of the last two days. Under such difficulties of ground the achievement is all the greater. The accuracy and rapidity of the artillery fire and the full advantage taken of it by the infantry were admirable.

From GOC, Fifth Army to GOC, V Corps
The Army Commander wishes to thank all ranks for their splendid efforts under most difficult conditions. The great

victory which they have won today will have very far-reaching effects. To this success all the troops engaged have contributed to the utmost of their power. Some have been more fortunate than others, but this always is the case in war and is to be expected. Great results have been achieved and the Army Commander's confidence in the leaders and troops has been more than justified.

From GOC, V Corps to GOC, 63rd (RN) Division
The Corps Commander congratulates commanders and troops including the heavy and field artillery on their magnificent and successful efforts today under trying conditions. The Commander-in-Chief has unofficially expressed his satisfaction.

From First Lord of the Admiralty to GOC, 63rd Division
Although the Admiralty are no longer responsible for the employment of the Naval Division, I follow their fortunes with great interest and have read with admiration the record of their gallantry in the recent success on the Ancre.

From GOC, 189th Infantry Brigade to All Units
The Brigadier has the very greatest pleasure in publishing the above telegrams. The Brigade has done splendidly and has added to the reputation made by the RND in the peninsula. While deploring the heavy casualties suffered by the Brigade, he congratulates the Officers, NCOs and Men of all units on their great achievement. He is very proud to command such a Brigade.[20]

One officer was not to receive congratulations. He was to be found wanting and would appear before a court martial.

References
  1. Public Record Office, Kew, Ref. WO 256/14: Haig's

Diaries.

2. Public Record Office, Kew, Ref. WO 32/5075: Nominal Roll of Officers, p. 10.

3. Imperial War Museum, Department of Documents: W.J. McCracken papers.

4. Public Record Office, Kew, Ref. ADM 137/3929.

5. Public Record Office, Kew, Ref. ADM 137/3065: Appendix 1: Nelson Battalion Order No. 50.

6. Public Record Office, Kew, Ref. ADM 137/3065: Appendix 2: Nelson Battalion Order No. 51.

7. Jerrold, Douglas, *The Great War: I Was There.*

8. Freyberg, Bernard, VC *A Linesman in Picardy*, chapter 2, pp. 11–15 (unpublished).

9. Liddle Collection, University of Leeds: J. Hall, Hood/Howe, Tape 387, November, 1976.

10. Public Record Office, Kew, Ref. ADM 137/3065: Appendix 1: Nelson Battalion Order No. 50, p. 122.

11. Public Record Office, Kew, Ref. ADM 137/3065: Nelson Battalion War Diary.

12. Public Record Office, Kew, Ref. WO 95/3112: Report of Operations, 189th Brigade.

13. Liddle Collection, University of Leeds: J.E. Frazer, RND Hawke, Ref. 201, February, 1974.

14. Public Record Office, Kew, Ref. ADM 137/3065: Nelson Battalion War Diary.

15. Liddle Collection, University of Leeds: W.E. Bland, Nelson Battalion, Ref. 436, March, 1977.

16. Liddle Collection, University of Leeds: J. Hall, Hood/Howe, Tape 387, November, 1976.

17. Imperial War Museum, Department of Documents: Thomas MacMillan.

18. Liddle Collection, University of Leeds: Brigadier R.B. Rackham, Tape 108, April 1972.

19. Public Record Office, Kew, Ref. WO 95/3112: Report of Operations, 189th Brigade.

20. Public Record Office, Kew, Ref. ADM 1367/3065: Nelson Battalion War Diary.

CHAPTER THREE

Court Martial

The first dated document in Dyett's court-martial file is the charge sheet (ref B2) which was signed by Lieutenant-Commander E.W. Nelson, the officer in charge of the Nelson Battalion; it is dated 19 December, 1916. He set out and signed the charges, as follows:

First Charge AAs. 12[1][a]	The accused, Temporary Sub-Lieutenant Edwin Leopold Arthur Dyett RNVR, an officer of the Nelson Battalion, 63rd Division, is charged when on active service deserting His Majesty's Service
	in that he
	in the field on the 13th November 1916, when it was his duty to join his battalion, which was engaged in operations against the Enemy, did not do so, and remained absent from his battalion until placed under arrest at Englebelmer on the 15th November, 1916.
Alternative Charge AA.S.40.	Conduct to the prejudice of good order and Military discipline
	in that he
	in the field on the 13th November 1916 did not go up to the front line when it was his duty to do so.

On 22 December, 1916, at General Headquarters of the British armies in France, by order of General Sir D. Haig, GCB, KCIE, KCVO, ADC, Army form A47 was completed for the assembly of a field general court martial. This form was to state that in the opinion of the Commander-in-Chief, British Armies in France, there was not present an officer authorized by warrant from the Admiralty to convene a general court martial. It listed the president and members.

There were under the control of the Judge Advocate General's Office four different types of court martial: general court martial, field general court martial, general regimental court martial and district or garrison court martial. The general court martial and field general court martial, to which Dyett was to be subject, were the army's highest tribunals. They were the only courts to have jurisdiction over commissioned officers. It required a warrant from the Crown or by specially appointed deputies such as the Commander-in-Chief. It was required that a Judge Advocate be present and that the court should consist of not less than five commissioned officers. Upon conviction the file had to be submitted to the Judge Advocate General's Office to ensure that the sentence and findings were legal. Once this had been confirmed the sentence was subject to confirmation, mitigation, remission, or commutation by the Sovereign or by the deputy who issued the warrant.

The trial was set for 10am on 26 December, 1916, at Champneuf, France, the President being Brigadier-General S.F. Metcalfe, DSO RA, officer commanding 18th Division RA. The members were:

Major (T/Lieut.-Col.) C.T. Martin, 2nd Battalion, Highland Light Infantry.

Major F.R. Day, 8th Battalion, Norfolk Regiment.

Major H.P.M. Berney-Fickling, 8th Battalion, Norfolk Regiment.

Major L.W. Miller RMLI, 2nd Battalion, Royal Marines.

Captain (T/Major) E.A. Winter, 23rd Battalion, Royal Fusiliers.

Before proceedings could get fully underway it was found

that Captain (T/Major) E.A. Winter, not having held his commission for the required period, had to be replaced by one of the two reserve officers, in this case Captain (A/Lieutenant-Colonel) J.S. Collings-Wells of the 4th Battalion, Bedford Regiment. The Judge Advocate was to be Captain J.S. Griffith-Jones of the 10th Battalion, South Wales Borderers (a barrister before the war).[1]

The Prosecutor was Sub-Lieutenant Herbert Slade Strickland, born 10 February, 1885. He had taken a commission as a Temporary Sub-Lieutenant RNVR at Crystal Palace on 6 June, 1915, moving on to Blandford on 3 September of that year. By 16 May, 1916, he had embarked at Mudros to land at Marseilles on 22 May, 1916, with the Nelson Battalion. After the court martial he was wounded in May, 1917, and killed in action on 3 September, 1918.[2]

It appears that Dyett could find no suitable person to defend him from his own Battalion, so Sub-Lieutenant Cecil Cameron Trevanion was chosen. He had been articled to one Arthur Henry Trevanion from 3 July, 1900, for a period of five years, to be admitted as a solicitor in January, 1912.[3] With regard to war service, he had been promoted from the ranks, having been a private with Princess Patricia's Canadian Light Infantry, at the age of 35 years and 9 months. He was commissioned as a Temporary Sub-Lieutenant with the RNVR at Crystal Palace on 30 November, 1915, transferring to Blandford by 15 April of the following year. He joined the Hawke Battalion of the Royal Naval Division. Later in the war he was wounded by a gas shell on 21 October, 1917, a wound that was thought to be lethal, but this was not so, and he became a revolver instructor at Aldershot, with the 2nd Reserve Battalion. He left the RND on 26 October, 1918, for sea service.[4]

The charges were read to the accused, who pleaded not guilty to both. With this the proceedings began. It was the president's task to take down the witnesses' evidence in longhand.[5]

First witness for the Prosecution

Lieutenant-Commander E.W. Nelson, Nelson Battalion

Edward William Nelson had been a Lieutenant in the Hood Battalion and saw action at Gallipoli, with such fellow officers as Bernard Freyberg, Patrick Shaw-Stewart, Denis Browne, Charles Lister and F.S. 'Cleg' Kelly. He had been the back-up to Bernard Freyberg when he made his historic swim in the Gulf of Saros on 25 April, 1915, in order to confuse the Turks. He was chosen, according to his Commanding Officer, Lieutenant-Colonel A.C. Quilter, because he was an extremely cool and reliable officer.[6] Before the war he had been the biologist on Scott's Antarctic Expedition.[7] He joined the Nelson Battalion on 24 May, 1916, in France and was to terminate his service in the Royal Naval Division on 16 May, 1917, when he went to *President*.[8]

> On 13 November, 1916, I was in command of the officers of the Nelson Battalion who were not taken into action with the Battalion at the commencement of operations. We were then stationed at Hédauville. In consequence of orders I received that day from the 63rd RN Divisional Headquarters I detailed Lieutenant Truscott and the accused to report to Brigade Headquarters. I personally gave these orders to both these officers and told them that a car was waiting to take them up at Divisional Headquarters.
>
> I saw both these officers leave in this car. The accused appeared to be quite nervous when I gave him these orders.

Cross-examined by accused's counsel
I have known the accused since about June last. I have been able, during the 5 months that the accused has been in my Battalion, to form an opinion of his capabilities as an officer.

My opinion of the accused's capabilities as an officer up to 13 November, 1916, was that he was a very poor one.

His authority in command over men was not good. Before 13 November the accused did approach me with a request for transference to sea service and the question as to his capabilities in the firing line was then raised by the accused.

Accused told me that he was of a very nervous temperament and that he thought that he was not fitted for the firing line.

I had no other officers available to go up to the firing line on 13 November. Sub-Lieutenant Cowans and Sub-Lieutenant Strickland were not available as they were employed on special duty. Sub-Lieutenant Redmond was not under my command doing duty at the time with the Divison. Sub-Lieutenant Walker was our Transport Officer, so he was not available. Sub-Lieutenant Truscott and accused were the only two officers available to be sent forward.

I felt some apprehension about sending the accused up into the firing line.

I had to send two officers and these were the only two available.

I had some misgivings about the accused. I had not the same confidence in him as in Lieutenant Truscott.

Re-examined by the Prosecutor
I thought the accused would carry out my orders, but I had misgivings as to his possible behaviour.

The evidence was read to the witness, who then withdrew.[9]

Second witness for the Prosecution

Lieutenant Cyril Alfred Truscott, Nelson Battalion
Truscott had become a Sub-Lieutenant on 19 January, 1915, at Crystal Palace. By 28 March, 1916, he had gained promotion as a temporary Lieutenant with the Nelson Battalion. He embarked at Mudros on 16 May, 1916, landing at Marseilles by the 22nd of that month. He died of wounds on 23 April, 1917, at Gavrelle.[10]

34

On 13 November, 1916, I received orders from Lieutenant-Commander Nelson. In compliance with these orders I joined the accused at Divisional HQ and drove in a car towards Brigade Headquarters. Brigade HQ was at that time in a trench called Charles Street, between the villages of Mesnil and Hamel.

On our arrival at the Brigade HQ I went into the HQ dug-out while the accused remained just outside it. Here as . . . [papers unclear] for both of us.

I there received certain orders from Brigadier-General L.F. Phillips which I communicated to the accused. I told the accused 'that the Brigadier has said that we (i.e. he and I) were to go and join the Battalion which had last been heard of in the GREEN LINE,' GREEN LINE was a trench on the Beaucourt side of Station Road: GREEN LINE is represented on the map I now produce by the blue pencil line. [The map was then marked 'Y' and signed by the President and attached to the proceedings.]

I showed the accused the position of GREEN LINE on my map as we were going up to join the Battalion in compliance with Brigadier-General Phillips's orders.

At Beaucourt Station the accused and I met a large number of men following Lieutenant Herring up the road. The accused and Lieutenant Herring entered into a heated conversation.

I proceeded to make enquiries for my Battalion from men of the party and particularly asked if any of my own Battalion were present among them.

On finding 25 men of my own Battalion I took charge of them and marched them towards the GREEN LINE. I left the accused still arguing with Lieutenant Herring.

Lieutenant Herring was not an officer in our Battalion and I did not know him.

I gave the accused no orders for he belonged to another Company and I thought we should each be going to our respective Companies. I therefore left him.

I did not hear any of the conversation between the accused and Lieutenant Herring.

I did not see the accused again until about mid-day on 15 November at Englebelmer.

The accused appeared to be normal when he was with me on 13 November. I noticed nothing strange in his demeanour.

It was about 5.45pm when I saw the accused.

Cross-examined by accused's counsel
I saw no signs whatever of what is termed 'cold feet' or any tendency on the part of the accused to desert.

I gave the accused no orders. I merely communicated the General's orders to him.

The Prosecution declined to re-examine
The Court asked no questions, the witness's evidence was read to him and he withdrew.[11]

Third Witness for the Prosecution

Brigadier-General Lewis Francis Phillips

General Officer Commanding 189th Infantry Brigade

From becoming a 2nd Lieutenant on 9 July, 1890, with the KRRC he had been steadily promoted and, from April, 1901, to February, 1902, was Assistant Provost Marshal in South Africa, later to be Assistant Military Secretary to the General Officer Commanding Ireland, and GSO (2) Northern Ireland, Northern Command. In the First World War he became Brigadier Commanding 70th Brigade from September to November, 1915. He took over 189th Brigade on 26 May, 1916.[12]

My advance Brigade Headquarters on 13 November, 1916, were about half a mile south-west of Hamel.

I was in command of the 189th Infantry Brigade on 13 November and the accused's Battalion was part of my Brigade.

My HQ on that day were in a dug-out off a communication trench. About 1.30pm on 13 November

Lieutenant Truscott and another officer came to my dug-out. Lieutenant Truscott came into the dug-out and I gave him cast-iron orders which applied to both officers.

I saw two officers at my dug-out and I recognized Truscott, but I cannot say who the other officer was.

On 15 November my Brigade came out of the line and we moved to Englebelmer. Owing to information that I had received I sent for the accused.

I questioned the accused and, as a result of his answers, I ordered the accused to be placed under arrest.

Neither the accused or any other officer of the Nelson Battalion reported to me at my Brigade HQ on 13 or 14 November after I had sent Lieutenant Truscott away. I first saw the accused on 15 November at Englebelmer after we had come out of the trenches.

Cross-examined by accused's counsel
I had no way of knowing whether Lieutenant Truscott communicated my orders to the accused.

I do not know whether the accused was the other officer who came to my dug-out with Lieutenant Truscott.

I placed the accused under arrest because of information that had been given to me and because of his unsatisfactory explanations.

The court asked no questions, the witness's evidence was read to him and he withdrew.

Fourth witness for the Prosecution

Captain A.R. Bare, Staff Captain, 189th Brigade, 63rd (RN) Division

On 13 November last about 1.30pm I was on duty at Brigade HQ in Charles Street Trench, when Lieutenant Truscott reported at the dug-out. I saw and spoke to the accused, who was in the upper dug-out at the same time.

I gave the accused no orders, nor did I hear any being given to him in the dug-out.

I next saw the accused at Englebelmer on the morning of 15 November, 1916. At the time the Nelson Battalion, to which the accused belonged, were in the line. They were not at Englebelmer. He had made no report to me.

When I saw the accused on 15 November, I immediately ordered him to report at Brigade HQ. It was then between 10 and 11 am.

Cross-examined by accused's counsel

I had previously known that the Brigadier had received a note from Lieutenant Herring concerning the accused's conduct.

The prosecution declined to re-examine. The court asked no questions. The evidence was read to him, and the witness withdrew.[13]

Fifth witness for the Prosecution

Sub-Lieutenant John Leigh Herring, Drake Battalion, RND

He had been promoted at Blandford from the rank of a Petty Officer to that of a Sub-Lieutenant on 29 November, 1915. He landed at Marseilles on 9 August, 1916, from Alexandria, which he had left seven days before. Later, in France, he was wounded by gun shot on 23 April, 1917. There is no doubt that he was a brave man, as he was awarded the Military Cross for conspicuous gallantry and devotion to duty, when he led his men in an attack during which they had to be reorganized when obstructed by wire and under heavy fire. He followed this up by leading bombing parties with great bravery and skill, until he was wounded. It was not until 12 October that he was fit for service, to be wounded again in March, 1918, by a gas shell. By 13 July he had recovered sufficiently to be transferred to the 2nd Reserve Battalion, where he remained until he was demobilized at Crystal Palace on 17 June, 1919, with a gratuity for his wounds.[14]

On 13 November last I was attached to the 189th Brigade Headquarters. I was in charge of the ammunition supply at Hamel, where I had my dumps. I was responsible that the ammunition was sent up from these to the firing line.

About 4.30pm or 5pm I saw the accused and Sub-Lieutenant Truscott at Beaucourt Station.

I knew the accused before, as I came out from England in the same draft with him.

Just before Lieutenant Truscott and the accused came up I had taken charge of 200 men, whom I found to be retiring. I had ordered them to 'about turn'. I made back towards the firing line. I realized that these men had no business to be retiring.

When Lieutenant Truscott came up to me and inquired for his Battalion I told him to take charge of the 200 men and to take them back to the firing line with him. I gave him this order as an order and he took the majority of the party off to the left.

[At this point in the court-martial file appears a margin note in pencil – 'In the Navy does a Sub-Lt give orders to a Lt?']

I then saw the accused and said to him: 'You go in the rear of those men and follow Truscott.'

The accused then replied: 'I am not the senior officer and I find such chaos here. I think I had better go back and report to the Brigade.'

I then went back to Hamel Dump and I noticed that the accused followed me. On arrival at my dump I at once wrote a message concerning the accused to the Staff Captain.

I did not see the accused until I got back to Arquèves about 15 November.

At the time that the accused and Truscott came up to me there was some confusion owing to the retirement of these men without any officer and there was a certain amount of shelling of the road going on. There was no attack actually proceeding at the time.

Accused appeared as if he expected to find his Battalion and he expected to report to his Battalion. The accused did not seem to grasp the situation. He was not agitated or frightened.

When I told the accused to follow Lieutenant Truscott, he appeared to resent it. He told me he was going to report at Brigade HQ, that he knew where the HQs were as he had just come from there.

Cross-examined by accused's counsel

Lieutenant Truscott is not accurate if he said that he merely took 25 men with him.

I was engaged on the Headquarters Staff and therefore I felt myself justified in ordering Lieutenant Truscott and the accused. Under the circumstances I felt myself justified in giving the order, though my particular and special duty had reference to communications and information only.

Had Lieutenant Truscott behaved in the same manner as the accused did, I would have reported him.

Q: Had Lieutenant Truscott disobeyed your order, would you have reported him?

A: Yes, under the circumstances I consider I had authority to order my senior officer.

I reported to the Staff Captain in writing 'that I had given orders to the accused to take some stragglers forward and that he had refused'.

There was not a great deal of confusion at the spot where I was, though there was a great deal of confusion elsewhere owing to units having got mixed up.

I do not consider that the accused was afraid.

Accused was not in my opinion deserting in the face of the enemy. In my opinion accused was going back to Headquarters to report that he found the place in a state of chaos.

Q: Are the relations between you and the accused all

that can be desired?

A: I have no personal animosity against the officer.

Q: Then why did the altercation take place between you and the accused immediately you met?

A: He appeared to resent my giving him an order.

Herring was then re-examined by the Prosecutor

I certainly should have reported Lieutenant Truscott if he had left the men where they were and followed me back.

The court asked no questions. His evidence was read to the witness and he then withdrew.[15]

Sixth witness for the Prosecution

Sub-Lieutenant Ernest Victor George Gardner, Nelson Battalion.

He had joined the Royal Naval Division at Crystal Palace on 10 March, 1915. In the battle on the Ancre he had been wounded, but remained on duty. As a result he was awarded the Military Cross for gallantry and devotion to duty. Later, on 8 May, 1917, he was to gain promotion to full Lieutenant, to be wounded again on 20 October of that year, with a severe wound to his hand and right shoulder. By March, 1918, he was listed as unfit for further service.[16]

I am a Company Commander in the Nelson Battalion.

On 13 November last I was present with my Battalion throughout an attack on the enemy which took place that day.

We first advanced from our own front line to the green line, which is behind the German third lines. About mid-day we had moved forward from green line trench to a position which we occupied about 150 yards south-west of Beaucourt. The Battalion remained in this position until about 4pm in the afternoon, when we moved back via Redoubt Alley to the extreme right of green line and dug ourselves in, in a position about 300 yards east of green line.

At 4pm I was the only officer of the Nelson Battalion who was present. I reported to Colonel Freyberg of the Hood Battalion about 5pm and it was on his instructions that I dug in extending his left flank. Our left was then in the air.

About 6pm Lieutenant Truscott joined me with a party of men, chiefly of the Nelson Battalion. He had about 40 to 50 men with him. Lieutenant Truscott, being the senior officer, then took over the command of the Battalion from me.

The Battalion remained in this last-named position until 5pm on the afternoon of 14 November, when we moved to a position about 50 yards in the rear.

We left this position about 2am on the morning of 15 November, when we were relieved.

The Battalion then retired to the original German front line and we remained here until 10.15am on the 15th when we marched back to Englebelmer and arrived there between 1 and 2 pm.

I never left the Battalion from and including 13 to 15 November and during the whole of the operations that took place on and between these dates I never saw the accused. The accused was absent from the Battalion during the whole of the period. I was the sole officer with the Battalion from about midday on the 13th until Lieutenant Truscott arrived about 6pm that evening. I did not see the accused until the evening of the 15th at Hédauville.

The court asked no questions. His evidence was read to him and he then withdrew.

Seventh witness for the Prosecution

AB (Acting Petty Officer) H.C. Aimes [the name is not clear on the file]

On 13 November I accompanied Sub-Lieutenant Herring as his assistant. I remember seeing Lieutenant Herring and the accused talking to each other near Beaucourt Station.

I overheard Lieutenant Herring tell Lieutenant Truscott, who was also present, to take charge of about 200 men and take them up to the firing line. I also heard Lieutenant Herring tell the accused who was with Lieutenant Truscott 'To give Lieutenant Truscott a hand with some of the men'. I cannot remember the exact words used but I have related the effect.

The accused did not carry out Lieutenant Herring's instructions. He turned to Lieutenant Herring and said, 'I cannot take charge among all this chaos and disorder. I will return to Brigade for orders.'

I next saw the accused turn in the direction of Brigade Headquarters. I last saw him in Hamel Dump.

The accused did not appear to grasp the situation when Lieutenant Herring told him to go with Lieutenant Truscott.

Cross-examined by accused's counsel

The accused appeared to resent taking an order from Lieutenant Herring.

Lieutenant Herring's duties that day, as far as I know, were confined to the supplying of ammunition.

Accused did not look as if he was afraid or in a funk. He looked as if he wanted to get out of it. *[This last comment could well be the answer that killed Dyett, coming as it did from a junior rank. In the file there is a heavy red line under the remark.]*

Accused said he was going back to Brigade HQ for orders, as he found everything in such a state of chaos.

The Prosecution declined to re-examine. The court asked no questions. His evidence was read to him and he withdrew.[17]

Eighth witness for the Prosecution

Lieutenant Bernard Dangerfield, Nelson Battalion

He had received his commission on 1 April, 1915, at Crystal Palace. As an officer of the Nelson Battalion he had gone out with the Mediterranean Expeditionary Force on 29 June 1915: by 20 October he was suffering from fever at Malta. Disembarking at Marseilles on 22 May, 1916, he gained promotion to a Temporary Lieutenant eight days later. During the Battle of the Ancre he had been wounded but remained on duty, and he was later awarded the Military Cross. On 18 May, 1917, he ended his service with the Division and was posted to the Royal Naval Air Service.[18]

> On 15 November about 1 o'clock I met the Battalion coming down from the German front-line system. I collected the Battalion in the neighbourhood of the German original front line and placed the men into dug-outs. They had just been relieved.
>
> About 10.20am I was in charge of half of the Battalion, and proceeded from the trenches to Englebelmer.
>
> On arrival at Englebelmer almost the first person that I saw was the accused. He was standing at the gate of No. 79 Billet, which was the HQ of the Battalion. About an hour later I saw Lieutenant Truscott in charge of the rest of the Battalion march into Englebelmer.

The accused's counsel declined to cross-examine. The court asked no questions. His evidence was read to him and he withdrew.

With Dangerfield's evidence the prosecution's case was closed. The court had asked no questions, no doubt or necessity for clarification had sprung to mind. There was no intelligent, probing enquiry, just acceptance of what was placed before them. There was no darting intervention by the President, as there might be by a Civil High Court Judge. Now it was the time for the defence to state its case. No doubt the court was wondering what Dyett's reply might be. The President of the Court, Brigadier S.F. Metcalfe, asked the following questions from the blue court-martial form, part D.

> *The President*: Do you apply to give evidence yourself as a witness?
> *Dyett*: No.
> *The President*: Do you intend to call any other witness in your defence?
> *Dyett*: No.
> *The President*: Have you anything to say in your defence?
> *Dyett*: I do not wish to say anything at all.

So there we have it: Edwin Dyett was not to put up a defence; he was leaving his destiny in the hands of the court. The prosecutor, Sub-Lieutenant Strickland, got up and addressed the court.

> Gentlemen,
>
> I had not intended saying anything at all. Having regard, however, to the evidence that has been adduced, I should like to point out that, even if the accused did not receive any definite orders to go up to join his Battalion, it was his duty to do so under the circumstances he found to be existing on his arrival at Beaucourt Station.

With this Sub-Lieutenant Cecil Trevanion spoke for the defence.
A summary of the speech is as follows:

> The accused is of a highly neurotic temperament and has for a long time felt himself unfit for occupying the

position of an officer over troops in the field. He was for five years an apprentice in the Mercantile Marine and, since his entry into the Naval Division in June, 1915, has made four separate applications for transfer into the Navy or Royal Naval Reserve. The applications were made to his respective commanding officers at the Crystal Palace, Blandford Camp, Lemnos and finally to his present OC ten days before the advance of the Naval Division on 13 November.

His present OC in his evidence admitted this application for transfer and also that the accused at the same time stated that his nerves prevented him from taking an active part in an advance and begged to be kept at the base as he had no confidence in his powers of leadership.

Accused's Officer Commanding also admitted that, had he not been called upon by the Division for two reinforcing officers, he would never have sent accused up to the front and, when he had started, had serious misgivings as to his possible demeanour and conduct. It is my contention that, after receiving final instructions from Brigade HQ, the accused in company with Lieutenant Truscott would have made a direct advance to the green line in search of his Battalion [the Nelson], had not the orders of Sub-Lieutenant Herring confused the issue. Lieutenant Truscott picked up a few men and searched for his Battalion; the contrary orders of Sub-Lieutenant Herring – to take control of a party of men – confused the issue and the accused, being confused as to what he should do, proceeded back in the direction of Brigade HQ for orders, as he was astounded at the terrible state of chaos which existed in the line.

Both Sub-Lieutenant Herring and the Petty Officer admit that the accused was not showing any signs of fear, but seemed unable to grasp the situation.

The accused in the darkness lost his way and, after spending the night in the dug-out, reported at Englebelmer to Lieutenant-Commander Egerton RNVR – the representative there of the 189th Brigade – who asked him if he wished to go to Headquarters, which the accused declined, stating that he would await the arrival of his Battalion.

The charge of desertion has not the slightest support of the evidence of any witness.

The accused's conduct throughout showed great lack of initiative in not at once grasping the altered instruction, and his return to Brigade HQ was for further enlightenment.

Now it was the turn of the Judge Advocate to sum up. Captain J.S. Griffith-Jones first read to the court the charges. In dealing with the first charge of desertion he referred to *The Manual of Military Law*, page 18, paras 13 & 16.

As to the alternative charge, he advised that the court would use their military knowledge to determine whether the acts complained of in the charges, if proved, amounted to such conduct as was prejudicial to both good order and military discipline.

The Judge Advocate then reviewed the facts and evidence, calling particular attention to the orders given to the accused by Lieutenant Truscott and Lieutenant Truscott's and Sub-Lieutenant Herring's evidence. As to defence – if the court think accused's neurotic and nervous condition to be such as to make it impossible for him to perform his duty – if such duty is established – they will [wording on the file is worn and unclear here] such justification for his conduct and against.

In support of this contention to Lieutenant-Commander E.W. Nelson, Sub-Lieutenant Herring and AB H.C. Aimes [name here also not clear on the court papers] 'Not in a funk'.

On the other [again papers not clear] no medical evidence had been called.

Accused did not report to the Brigade HQ Staff Captain or the General. He remained absent over the 14th and was next seen on 15 November awaiting the Battalion's return to billets.

The Judge Advocate laid stress on the question of intention. Is the court satisfied that accused intended to annex some particular and important duty? The court must be satisfied on this before finding desertion. Mistake or error of judgment does not amount to intent.

With this advice the court was closed for the consideration of the findings. The blue court-martial form section E, parts 10 and 11 shows clearly the verdict:

> The court find that the accused, Temporary Sub-Lieutenant Edwin Leopold Arthur Dyett RNVR, an officer of the Nelson Battalion, 63rd Division is Guilty of the First Charge but not Guilty of the Alternative Charge.

The court then re-opened: evidence of character and conduct was to be heard. Lieutenant Dangerfield, the Acting Adjutant of the Nelson Battalion, was again called and duly sworn.

The President:	Have you any evidence to produce as to the character and and particulars of service of the accused?
Dangerfield:	I produce particulars of the character and service of the accused.

The following statement was then read, marked 'Z', and signed by the President.

1 The accused has not been previously convicted.
2 The accused is not under sentence.
3 The accused has been in close arrest awaiting trial on the present charge 42 days.
4 The present age of the accused is 21 years.
5 The date of his commission is June 24th 1915.
6 The accused is in possession or entitled to no military decoration or military reward which the court can forfeit.

The President:	Is the accused person named in the statement which you read?
Dangerfield:	Yes.
The President:	Have you compared the contents of the above statement with the regimental books?
Dangerfield:	Yes.
The President:	Are they true extracts from the regimental books?
Dangerfield:	Yes.

The accused's counsel declined to cross-examine. The court sentenced the accused, the sentence being: Death. Temporary Sub-Lieutenant Edwin Leopold Arthur Dyett RNVR, an officer of the Nelson Battalion, 63rd Division to suffer death by being shot.

However, the court recommended mercy on the following grounds:

1 He is very young and has no experience of active operations of this nature.

2 The circumstances – growing darkness, heavy shelling and the fact that men were retiring in considerable numbers – were likely to affect seriously a youth, unless he had a strong character.

Signed at Champneuf, France this Twenty-Sixth Day of December 1916[19]

References

1. Public Record Office, Kew, ref. ADM 156/24.
2. MoD, Whitehall Library, Royal Naval Division Books ROS 182 & 182: Officers' Service 1914–1919, Vols 1 & 2.
3. The Law Society letter to L.G. Sellers, 30 December, 1993, ref. PSD/JP/CJC.

4. MoD, Whitehall Library (as above).
5. Public Record Office, Kew, ref. ADM 156/24.
6. Public Record Office, Kew, ref. WO 95/4290: Report by Lieutenant-Colonel A.C. Quilter, 26 April 1915.
7. Murray, Joseph, interviews with L.G. Sellers.
8. MoD, Whitehall Library (as above).
9. Public Record Office, Kew, ref. ADM 156/24.
10. MoD, Whitehall Library (as above).
11. Public Record Office, Kew, ref. ADM 156/24.
12. Froom, Tony, letter to L.G. Sellers, 1 January 1994. ref. 14.
13. Public Record Office, Kew, ref. ADM 156/24.
14. MoD, Whitehall Library (as above).
15. Public Record Office, Kew, ref. ADM 156/24.
16. MoD, Whitehall Library (as above).
17. Public Record Office, Kew, ref. ADM 156/24.
18. MoD, Whitehall Library (as above).
19. Public Record Office, Kew, ref. ADM 156/24.

CHAPTER FOUR

Awaiting the Verdict

To obtain Dyett's version of events one has to go back to
the period before the court martial, when he was awaiting
developments since being placed under close arrest. After
being kept in limbo for four weeks, on 13 December he
wrote to a friend:

> We went up the line and took over the right sector for
> four days; there we were relieved and returned to our
> billets, and my Company, with others, during the night
> took up our position, and things went fairly well until
> late in the morning, when I was detailed to go and
> replace casualties – you were in that scrap, so there is no
> need to explain how many. I crossed no-man's-land
> later in the afternoon, but could not find a man belong-
> ing to my unit. My companion went off with a crowd
> we met, but as I still held hope of finding the Company,
> I rambled about and lost touch with everybody, and my
> nerves, not being strong, were completely strung up. I
> met another officer, who says he ordered me to join up
> with the party, but this I did not do, but wandered about
> still looking for my own unit. In the meantime this
> gentleman went back and sent a startling message of
> sorts to BHQ, with result that they are trying to kick me
> out of it, but up to now [13 December] the evidence
> given is not strong enough to cause a 'sitting'. And that
> is what happened to me in the biggest advance – luck,
> isn't it? It makes me sick to think of it, and they have

now kept me a month hanging on. I am hoping for news any day now, and if there is nothing in it do not see why I should worry my people by telling them. Now I have all the Company letters to censor, so please excuse more.

By Christmas Eve, some six weeks after the battle, he was still waiting, but now with the ill-judged belief that a court martial was unlikely. He wrote on this day as follows:

I hear that you are worrying about me more than is necessary. I will explain my present situation so as to relieve your mind. I was surplus, and was sent off at five minutes' notice. I went up with another officer of my Battalion who was senior by one ring. We reported our-selves at Brigade Headquarters as instructed by our Lieutenant-in-Command. At that time they had lost touch with the Battalion, so we waited for an hour or so in their dug-out awaiting orders, which we got – at least, the other man got them, and then after a lot of trouble I got them to tell me what they were and we proceeded towards Boche overland. There was consid-erable hostile artillery, gas shells and tear shells falling all round us, and snipers were all over the place; we had very narrow shaves more than once. We could not find our units and rambled about.

When it was dark, we met a body of men with an officer in charge; they were wanted by Colonel Freyberg VC [Hood Battalion]; there was much confusion and disorder going on, and my nerves became strung up to the highest extreme. I found that my companion had gone off somewhere with some men. The officer who was leading the party we met was my 'one and only enemy', so we were not polite to each other, and as he is junior to me I practically ignored him except for telling him I was going back to BHQ, which I had left an hour or two before in daylight, but finding those places was not as easy a matter as I thought, with the result that I got lost for the second time. I found an NCO

1. Temporary Sub-Lieutenant Edwin Leopold Arthur Dyett.

2. Edwin Dyett with his father 'later in the First World War to be Chief Naval Transport Officer at Liverpool Naval Base' (p.11).

3.Petty Officer, 63rd [RN] Division.

4. Machine Gun Section 63rd [RN] Division.

CAP BADGES

5. Nelson Battalion.

6. Anson Battalion.

7. Howe Battalion.

8. Hawke Battalion.

CAP BADGES

9. Drake Battalion.

10. Hood Battalion.

GO !

IT'S YOUR
DUTY LAD

JOIN TO-DAY

11. British recruiting poster.
12. German recruiting poster.

Deutsche
Frauen
arbeitet
im
Heimat-
heer!

Kriegsamtstelle
Magdeburg

of the old A Company – we rambled about until he fell down for want of sleep, but I managed to get him along. Later my voice was recognized by some more men of the A Company who were lost; they attached themselves to me, saying they also were looking for BH Quarters. BHQ, however, were not to be found that night. My nerves were completely gone and my head was singing. About then we came across a funk hole, and there we stayed. However, my 'enemy' had gone back behind his supports and sent a startling message to BHQ concerning me. I have been under close arrest ever since November 14th.

On November 8th I put in an application to the Commanding Officer telling him my reasons for wanting to return to sea on account of my nerves not being able to stand the strain. He told me he was just the same as I, so I let it slide at that, as I did not want everyone to say that I was trying to 'swing the lead' as others have done. I have obeyed orders, and that is all I care about it. Things are very one-sided just now, but as soon as I have my little say in the matter it will alter their colour altogether. Now that is as much as you can know of what happened as if you had found out yourself.[1]

However, the writer has found that there was another witness to Dyett's conduct, who didn't give evidence. He was an officer with the Hood Battalion who was badly injured and, as will be seen, had little sympathy for Dyett. Sub-Lieutenant J.H. Bentham writes:

Suddenly a shell burst among us and when the smoke had cleared I found my two runners killed, wounded myself through the thigh and maiming nearly all the remainder. I gave my map and instructions to an NCO and told him to carry on. He was killed just as he left me. This was at exactly 6.15am. We had certainly had a hectic half hour and now it was all over. One of my lads was wounded in the lung and was coughing up bright red blood and it wasn't long before he died. The remainder took what shelter we could in a crater as the enemy were plastering us with shells. Wave after wave of reinforcements passed us shouting, 'Got a blighty, lucky devil', etc. Then we got our first-aid packages and bandaged our wounds as best we could; my leg was pumping blood. At about 10am our Battalion Medical Officer McCracken came along and dressed our wounds. He poured iodine into my wound and told me that that would stop me laughing in church! He had to go with the Battalion but said some stretcher bearers would be along later. Lying with our backs to the front, we could see reinforcements coming over the brow of a hill at the rear, not far away hidden in an isolated pocket was a German machine gun, who took a terrible toll of those men as they showed against the sky line. I tried to crawl and ascertain where this devil could be, but it was too far away so I shouted until someone came along and I told him and sure enough shortly afterwards the gun stopped. I had given my morphine tablets to the more seriously wounded to deaden the pain, but soon the effects wore off and they started moaning with the pain. It was now afternoon and no one had come along. We opened our iron rations and had something to eat, those of us who could do so, but one poor lad with a shattered arm and smashed shoulder blade was praying to die and begged us to put him out of his misery. The afternoon dragged on and I realized that stretcher bearers would not find us in the dusk which came down. German shells were still dropping all round and we wondered if one would find us and finish us off.

My wound by now had set hard and numbed with cold I did all I could to cheer up the others. The night passed and it seemed a lifetime and we began to despair of being found at all as there was no signs of life what-soever. Dawn came and turned into day and then an officer I knew to be one of the reserves came along. He looked white and scared and asked me where the front line was. I told him it must be a long way now but he would jolly well soon recognize it when he got there. Off he went and I never saw him again, but that same officer was later shot for cowardice. He had deserted his support troops who, without an officer, never arrived in the front line. *John Bull* however without knowing the true facts made a great fuss about it and placards were headed 'Shot at Dawn' and 'Tragedy of Young Boy Officer'.

Another badly wounded boy died that morning and others were of the opinion that we should perish there, it was now over 24 hours since we were knocked out. Thank God it wasn't raining. Our iron rations were finished and at 2pm, exactly 36 hours after being hit, a party of German prisoners under a guard came along with stretchers.[2]

It is small wonder that Bentham had little compassion for Dyett. He had seen his men die in agony, a shocking death. If Dyett came across the injured party, after dawn, he seems to have done nothing to report the location of these injured men or speed up the stretcher bearers.

If, as according to his letter of Christmas Eve, he had come across some men and an NCO of A Company, why had he left the company of these men? If he was with them, why were they never called as witnesses? Sub-Lieutenant Trevanion, in his speech for the defence, states that Dyett lost his way in the darkness and, after spending the night in the dug-out, reported at Englebelmer to Lieutenant-Commander Egerton RNVR, the representative there of the 189th Brigade. It was said that Egerton asked if he wished to go to Headquarters; Trevanion states Dyett declined, saying he would await the arrival of his Battalion. Strangely, Egerton was not called as a witness. Why did this senior officer not order Dyett? When one knows the situation and the shortage of officers, this appears very strange. It must have been due to the fog of battle that Egerton was not aware of Sub-Lieutenant Herring's report to Brigade HQ concerning Dyett's conduct. Englebelmer is situated a few miles north-west of Mesnil.

It appears that Dyett waited about for the return of his

Battalion and was seen standing at the gate of a billet. This must have been on the morning of the 15th, as in the Judge Advocate's summing up he clearly states that the accused was absent over the 14th and was next seen on 15 November awaiting the Battalion's return to billets. Strangely, it is not made clear at the court martial what the situation was. Trevanion for the defence states:

> The accused, in the darkness lost his way and, after spending the night in the dug-out, reported at Englebelmer to Lieutenant-Commander Egerton.

This would clearly imply the night of the 13th/14th, and that he reported to Egerton on the 14th. The charge states: 'and remained absent from his battalion until placed under arrest at Englebelmer on the 15th November 1916'.

Even this is incorrect. He waited for his Battalion, who found him by the gate. He was later sent for by Brigadier-General L.F. Phillips, and questioned about his conduct. The Brigadier was not happy with his story and it was then and only then that Dyett was arrested.

There is one other small indication that Dyett might have been missing only one night before reporting to Egerton. In his letter of Christmas Eve he writes: 'I have been under close arrest ever since November 14th.' This is clearly wrong, but it could indicate that in his own mind he was aware that he only spent one night out on the battlefield.

Why was Dyett kept waiting so long for news of his court martial? There should in practice have been a preliminary hearing of the evidence, in order to decide if there was sufficient evidence to proceed with the matter. In his letter of 13 December Dyett states: 'the evidence given is not strong enough to cause a "sitting"'. He should have been supplied with a copy of the Summary of Evidence. The court-martial file contains no such item.

As we have seen, on Christmas Eve he was still waiting, but he would come before the court on Boxing Day. Even if we estimate that he wrote his Christmas Eve letter at noon, this would give him only 46 hours to prepare his defence. (This aspect will be considered further in a later chapter.)

The officer who defended Dyett was, strangely, not an officer of his own Battalion, but of the Hawke. As it transpired Dyett did not speak in his own defence. He fully intended to do so, as stated in his Christmas Eve letter: 'as soon as I have my little say in the matter it will alter their colour altogether'.

Why, therefore, did he remain silent? One reason could have been that Trevanion was extremely concerned about Dyett's nervous condition and feared that, by giving evidence, he would be likely to prejudice his case. It appears that his state of mind could not have been all that disturbed, as the defence obtained no medical evidence. The cards that Trevanion was to play were those of being unfit to be an officer in the field, having applied for release from the role on a number of occasions, and being confused by orders from Herring in the chaos of battle: and, with this defence, reliance on the sympathy of the court. In one way it worked. The court passed the death sentence, but with a strong recommendation for mercy. Judge Babington, who has studied all of the court-martial files at the Public Record Office and is an expert on the subject, states:

> The real fallacy of these cases was the sentencing. The court hadn't got the foggiest idea how to sentence. They were empowered to impose the death penalty or such lesser punishment as they deemed fit. And again and again they imposed the death sentence and illogically again and again they recommended mercy. The reason was that a lot of junior officers or fairly junior officers thought we will impose the death sentence and then when the papers are passed up to higher officers that they will put it right.[3]

That the fates were not kind to Dyett is clear; a chain of circumstances led inevitably to his court martial. The most unlucky coincidence was that the one officer he came across when going forward was Sub-Lieutenant John Herring, his one and only enemy in the Division. Apparently Dyett had caught this officer sneaking a woman into their training camp at Blandford, in Dorset.[4] This ill feeling must have rankled in Herring's mind, but would most likely not have been of any consequence as they were in different Battalions, and therefore would not normally come across each other. However, destiny took a hand when Herring was attached to the 189th Brigade Headquarters. As a result he appears to have obtained a somewhat inflated opinion of his position. Junior to Dyett, he still took it upon himself to order him to take men forward; not satisfied with this, he had also given orders to a full Lieutenant. (One can imagine Dyett's reaction.) As a result an altercation took place and, as Dyett writes, 'I practically ignored him'. Herring returned to his ammunition dump, no doubt in a state of righteous indignation, and made an immediate and highly derogatory report of Dyett's conduct. It is likely that Herring did not clearly foresee the probable result of his allegations.

Dyett's meeting with Herring must have been mind-blowing for the highly strung young officer. Having to steel himself against the falling shells, bullets, gas and gore was bad enough, but to find himself confronted by a hostile colleague, giving out orders, even though his junior, must have been the last straw. He followed Herring and was seen by the Petty Officer back at Hamel ammunition dump. He had come back a long way, since the Headquarters of the 189th Brigade was only half a mile south-west of Hamel. Why did Dyett not go there? Possibly by this time his anger had subsided, to be replaced by apprehension, knowing that Herring had no love for him and expecting that he would be true to his nature and report matters. What would he say? What could he do? No doubt he turned about once more, intending to find the front. But the confused conditions and fear became his master and were too strong. He got lost. Resignation set in and hopelessness took over. He was missing from his Battalion until, like a naughty schoolboy, he waited for them by a billet gate.

On four separate occasions the prisoner had made

application for transfer to sea and from the infantry. Such transfers were not unknown in the Royal Naval Division. This was the case on Gallipoli, and later on the Greek islands. Indeed, after the battle of 4 June, 1915, Commodore Oliver Backhouse, officer in charge of the 2nd Brigade, had applied for transfer to the naval artillery, when he fell out with Major-General Paris. On the islands, after the evacuation, petty officers and men had made written applications to the Admiralty, which were often granted. The last of Dyett's requests was to his Commanding Officer, a short time before the Battle of the Ancre. He had said that he was of a very nervous temperament and thought that he was not fitted for the firing line. According to Dyett, Commander Nelson replied that he was just the same, so he let it slide. It appears likely that Dyett's family connections were known in the Battalion. This must have been common knowledge when he joined the RND and was likely to have come up in conversation in the officers' mess. Armed with this information, would a commanding officer recommend a transfer? Would this indicate failure by Dyett's superiors or by himself in particular, in the eyes of the staff? Still, no mention of Dyett's family is to be found in the court-martial file. Was higher authority unaware? Was the information to be kept at local level only?

One never knows when one will be overcome by events. Dyett's time was in 1916. E.W. Nelson's time was to be when he was forty years of age. He was by then the Scientific Superintendent of the Marine Laboratory at the Bay of Nigg in Scotland. In the London Divorce Court his wife was granted a decree for restitution of conjugal rights. As a result she wrote to him pleading for him to return to her. He replied: 'If I believed that coming together again could possibly lead to anything but further unhappiness I would gladly agree.' The order made should have been obeyed within 14 days, but Nelson was found dead in his office in Aberdeen. Backbone is but a shield; time and circumstance have the last word.[5]

There are a number of other matters that need to be raised. When Sub-Lieutenant Herring gave his evidence his words were 'The accused did not seem to grasp the situation'. When AB (Acting PO) H.C. Aimes gave evidence he used exactly the same words. Now the evidence was taken down in long hand and was read to the witness and signed by him, before he stood down. It appears strange that this same wording was used by both officer and man. Apparently these witnesses had fully discussed their evidence and their answers. The same Acting Petty Officer was virtually to sign Dyett's death warrant with the words 'Accused did not look as if he was afraid or in a funk. *He looked as if he wanted to get out of it*' (my italics). Later these words were heavily underlined in red when higher echelons were considering if the sentence should be carried out.

Dyett was of the opinion that: 'Things are very one-sided just now'. Was he therefore given a fair trial – i.e. did he have time to produce an adequate defence? There is one other strange comment in Dyett's letter of Christmas Eve. He writes concerning the time that he and Lieutenant Truscott reported to Brigade Headquarters: 'so we waited for an hour or so in their dug-out awaiting orders, which we got – at least, the other man got them, and then *after a lot of trouble I got them to tell me what they were*' (my italics).

This appears to be inexcusable. Was there a set against Dyett by his brother officers? His commanding officer, in his evidence, considered him to be a very poor one, and that his authority in command was not good. Was he already something of an outcast and held back as the last resort? Why on earth should Dyett have been given so much trouble in finding out his orders? If this was the case, one can imagine how alone he must have been feeling, even without support. Therefore it is no wonder that he failed. Lieutenant-Colonel Freyberg of the Hood Battalion, who was the officer that Dyett was to have supported, wrote about the quality of officer that he picked to go forward with the attack:

We had, when we marched into the Somme battle area, some 52 officers, of unequal quality, and we knew that, when we marched out in a few weeks' time, only a third would remain. It was important that the Battalion should be officered by good men, both after as well as during the battle; and, as the complement of officers we were allowed to take into each assault was 20, we decided to take our 12 best and our 8 worst. The worst were all told why they were picked, and that they would have good men in front, and behind, to keep an eye on them; and often these officers, spurred on by the thought that they were undergoing a careful examination, excelled. They were given unstinted praise and recognition, and having once done well they seldom looked back.[6]

To go forward in this battle as a relief was an extremely daunting experience. Sub-Lieutenant Trevor Jacobs of the Hood Battalion, who likewise was ordered forward in support of Freyberg, writes:

Getting up there was a devil of a job, being enfiladed from either side and most of it being done in the open. Three of us going to another Brigade were blown up by a shell and another suffered the effects of a machine gun. I walked over very nonchalantly and did not even bother to double, just to show how cool I felt (I don't think). The real reason was to preserve my strength for later on. I did occasionally, when it became rather warm, flop into a shell hole, for a short respite. We eventually arrived at our destination. Of course we passed very many dead. And any number of stretchers.[7]

Now we come to probably the saddest aspect of the story. When Dyett met Herring at the railway station he was very near to the then front line, and the Nelson. At 5pm it was just 150 yards east of the green line, and later moved back another 50 yards. If this fateful meeting had not taken place, Dyett would, most likely, have continued, and might have blossomed and settled, as Freyberg's man management indicates. Fate proved decisive. The only person liable to destroy his confidence, stop his attempt forward and antagonize him was waiting. Dyett's number was up.

After the court martial the file went from J.S. Griffiths-Jones, the Judge Advocate of HQ Reserve Army, on 27 December to his superior, the Deputy Judge Advocate General and on to the Adjutant-General by the 28th. This was to check on the legality of the hearing. Once this was established, it was forwarded to the Fifth Army as follows:

> To Fifth Army
> Will you please forward your recommendations as to whether the sentence should be carried out or commuted and those of the Divisional and Corps Commander.
> 28/12/16   AAG for Adj. Colonel

> V Corps
> The Division did very well on the Ancre and behaved most gallantly. Added to this Sub-Lieut Dyett is very young and inexperienced. Beyond the above I know of no reason why the extreme penalty should not be exacted.
>   I recommend mercy.
>   C.D. Shute, Major-Gen.
>   Comder, 63rd (RN) Div.

> Fifth Army
> Forwarded. I see no reason why the sentence should not be carried out.
> 30 December 1916 C.M. Macob
>   Lieut-General
>   Commanding V Corps

> AG
> GHQ
> I recommend that the sentence be carried out. If a private had behaved as he did in such circumstances, it is highly probable that he would have been shot.
>   H Gough
>   General
> 31/12/16 Commanding Fifth Army

Field Marshal Douglas Haig was to write on the file on 2 January, 1917, one word: 'Confirmed'.[8]

Edwin Dyett's fate was sealed.

References

1. *John Bull*, 23 February, 1918.
2. Bentham, John Henry – taken from *A Young Officer's Diary* at the Liddle Collection, University of Leeds.
3. *The Times*, 20 August, 1983, 'Tragedy of the Young Officer who lost his way'.
4. Babington, Judge Anthony: from BBC Radio 4, 7.20pm, 16 September, 1993: 'Document'.
5. Imperial War Museum, Department of Documents: McCracken papers.
6. Freyberg, Bernard, VC *A Linesman in Picardy*, chapter 2, p. 9 (unpublished).
7. Imperial War Museum, Department of Documents, ref. 88/27/1: Sub-Lieutenant Trevor Jacobs.
8. Public Record Office, Kew, ref. ADM/156/24: court-martial file.

CHAPTER FIVE

As an Example

It was a great shock when I opened the file listing details of executions in the Great War. What I found amazed and deeply troubled me. There were the names, ages and details. I discovered that they were so young, so vulnerable and so alone. Part of the file was a tabular statement relating to men of the British Army who were sentenced by court martial to be shot. It listed 32 cases (a sample only of the 346 total – extracted for a later parliamentary enquiry). The youngest was 18, the oldest just 20 years and 11 months. In only three cases did the prisoner have the benefit of a prisoner's friend. These young men, on trial for their lives, went before their superiors without legal representation or assistance. The knowledge of this is horrific, and has deep implications.

Under the heading 'Remarks and particulars of character' were to be found the following:

19 years, 5 months	Until recently he has been a good soldier, and bore a good character, lately he seems to have lost his nerve.
[No accused's friend]	
19 years, 211 days	From the fighting point of view useless, goes to pieces under shelling, poor type. Character as soldier fairly satisfactory but has mostly

been in hospital.

[No accused's friend]

20 years, 6 months   Man was not a man who gave much trouble, neither was he in any sense a man whom one would pick out as a good man. Considered to be of poor intellect, not of much consideration as a fighting man.

[No accused's friend]

20 years, 5 months   Poor character lately since mother's death, before that no serious complaint.

[No accused's friend][1]

Some 346 men were executed between 1914 and 1919, the majority condemned to death had their sentences commuted.

Death sentences carried out

	Imperial	Colonial	Overseas	Chinese	Coloured	Followers	Total
Mutiny	2		1				3
Cowardice	15	2	1				18
Desertion	240		26				266
[incl 1 officer]							
Murder	15	1	3	10	3	5	37
[incl 2 officers]							
Striking officer	4	1			1		6
Disobedience	5						5
Sleeping at post	2						2
Quitting post	7						7
Casting away arms	1	1					2
	291	5	31	10	4	5	364[2]

Commuted death sentences

	Passed	Commuted	Carried out	% Carried out
Imperial troops	2690	2399	291	10.82
Colonial force	10	5	5	50
Overseas contingents	355	324	31	8.73
Native) Chinese	13	3	10	76.92
Labour)				
Corps) Coloured	4	–	4	100
Followers	8	3	5	62.5
	3080	2734	346	11.23[3]

The main offences which led to execution were desertion and cowardice. A War Office memorandum outlines the difference between these military offences:

> Cowardice is dealt with in section 4 (7) of the Army Act and is misbehaving before the enemy in such a manner as to show that the accused from an unsoldierlike regard for his personal safety in the presence of the enemy failed in respect of some military duty. The essence of the offence of cowardice is that it must occur 'before the enemy', that is to say actually in the presence of danger. Nowhere special intention of any kind forms an ingredient of the offence and it may, and indeed most frequently is, due to fear or failure of nerves.
>
> Desertion, which is dealt with in section 12 of the Army Act, is absence without leave with the intention either of never returning to the service at all or avoiding some particular onerous or dangerous service. If differs from cowardice in that it involves a definite and specific intention. It need not occur in the presence of any danger and is more likely to be the result of a calculating regard by a man for his own safety than cowardice which is inspired by fear in the presence of actual danger.
>
> There are some offences in which both the elements of cowardice and desertion are present; thus if a soldier in the presence of an enemy during the course of his engagement turns his back on the enemy and runs away

the act of turning his back on the enemy and starting to run away is cowardice. Any subsequent absence from the scene of danger with the intent of avoiding danger is desertion.[4]

The penalty of death for sleeping on post involves somewhat different considerations. It is no doubt true that, during the war, it was never found necessary to carry out the death penalty for this offence in France, but the sentence was actually passed in many cases, and it was always made clear that if such cases became numerous, it would be necessary to carry out the extreme penalty. It was, therefore, present to the mind of every sentry that there was definite risk of his being shot if he went to sleep, and this knowledge must have had a powerful effect in promoting vigilance. It is highly probable that if there had been no death penalty in reserve many more cases would have occurred, and serious risk of disaster might have been incurred. Two cases occurred in which the death penalty was carried out in another theatre of war.[5]

In fact courts martial dealing with capital offences were only the tip of the iceberg, as figures of Army courts martial between 1914 to 1919 show:

	4.8.14 to 30.9.14	1.10.14 to 30.9.15	1.10.15 to 30.9.16	1.10.16 to 30.9.17	1.10.17 to 30.9.18	1.10.18 to 30.9.19
Officers tried at home						
GCM	1	86	356	435	814	599
Officers tried abroad						
GCM	4	68	478	735	838	842
FGCM	1	17	15	58	141	159
Soldiers tried at home						
GCM	3	121	43	158	63	149
FGCM	33	279 [all Ireland]				
DCM	629	19,340	27,053	32,692	32,396	19,037

GCM	–	22	63	21	22	130
FGCM	52	14,743	30,295	32,830	41,668	30,357
DCM	90	877	721	1,058	1,284	820[6]

GCM: general court martial
DCM: district court martial
FGCM: field general court martial

When I was researching this book, it became clear to me that to be a member of a firing party was abhorrent, repugnant and a duty to be undertaken only with extreme reluctance. The act of taking the life of a member of one's Battalion, in cold blood, had long-term effects on those involved. Sudden prolonged and unexpected flash-back of that memory would unsettle officers and men alike. One wanted the event expunged from the mind and the scene to fade into oblivion.

Did it affect the general or staff officer who confirmed death or made recommendations to the same extent? Most likely the answer to this must be no. An analogy would be the bomber crew, flying over a city and removed from the horror of sudden death, in comparison with the infantryman who pushes the bayonet home. Confirming a death sentence cannot be compared with the close proximity of the firing party.

Julian Putkowski in his 1993 radio programme in the series 'Document' states:

> Senior military figures had to take a whole host of factors into consideration when deciding whether a sentence should be quashed. Far wider than the evidence provided at the courts martial. General Sir Anthony Farrar-Hockley has had a long and distinguished military career. He is also a military historian and an authority on the First World War. He's commanded a Division in war time and studied how other generals had had to make difficult decisions in the heat of battle. He believes there is no simple answer to what influenced a Divisional Commander.

General Sir Anthony Farrar-Hockley states:

> It would certainly be true that the personality of the
> Divisional Commander and in some cases the Corps
> Commander in this particular matter were of crucial
> importance. The Divisional or sometimes the Corps
> Commander was the superior military authority, that is
> the officer who put the final endorsement of the matter
> of sentence for final confirmation. There was therefore,
> and is in his hands always, the capability of mitigating
> the sentence. Now a man appointed Divisional Com-
> mander for the first time, beginning to receive such
> papers, may have found it a difficult matter to put down
> 'confirmed' and his signature to a sentence of death. I
> guess that it did not get more difficult, it probably got
> easier if circumstances convinced him that the object
> lesson of some individual execution would save lives or
> would save indeed more than lives but a local situation.[7]

There follow a number of accounts, from chaplains, an
officer, a private soldier, and medical officers. Battalion
chaplains had to play a part. But executions had a long-term
effect even on these men of God, as highlighted by a letter
by a Canon with the Guards Division. He writes:

> Shall I tell you of the terrible experience I have just gone
> through? It has just fallen to my lot to prepare a deserter
> for his death – that meant breaking the news to him,
> helping him with his last letters, passing the night with
> him on the straw of his cell, and trying to prepare his
> soul for meeting God; execution and burying him imme-
> diately. The shadow was just hanging over me when I
> wrote my last letter but I tried to keep it out. Monday
> night I was with him, Tuesday morning at 3.30 he was
> shot. He lay beside me for hours with his hand in mine.
> Poor fellow, it was a bad case, but he met his end
> bravely, and drunk in all I could teach him about God,
> his father, Jesus his saviour, and the reality of the for-
> giveness of sins. I feel a little shaken by it all, but my

nerves, thank God, have not troubled me. Everyone has been so kind who knew of the ordeal.[8]

A Chaplain to the Royal Fusiliers gives his account:

At the end of March a man who had deserted was caught, tried by Court Martial and sentenced to be shot. It was a bright spring morning when the Battalion was drawn up for his sentence to be promulgated. I had to prepare him for his tragic end, which he seemed not to realize himself. Whether his mind was deficient I do not know, but he seemed to be numbed, showing no signs of fear or any emotion.

Early in the morning I went with him and the escort and there at one side of a field the firing party stood. The man's eyes were blindfolded and as I turned away and went apart the volley rang out and the poor lad passed to his account. I felt that he was certainly not so much to blame as another man, the leader of a little gang of men who had deserted and hidden themselves at Poperinghe. He was the man who ought to have been shot, for he gave this boy away and escaped himself.

In 1918 this man himself was captured and sentenced to death, but was released and given another chance on the ground that at some other time he had acquitted himself gallantly in action. Yet I fear the leniency was misplaced, for at the first opportunity he escaped again and gave himself up to the Germans and after the armistice was returned as a prisoner of war.[9]

For some the ordeal was to prove just too much to bear, as shown by the following description by an officer of the Suffolk Regiment when a number of foreign nationals had to be shot, after being found guilty of espionage:

I was second in command of the Company. . . . I could fight in the ordinary way, but [shooting] people in cold blood was beyond me. So I did my best to pull strings so I didn't have to shoot these people.

70

There was another chap, much older than me, who had lost a son during the war – he had got killed. I said all sorts of things. 'Wouldn't it be a good thing if he had his revenge on these people.' I was so persistent that this poor chap was ordered – I was told to order him to take this shooting. I was sorry for him, but really there are some things that you can do and others you can't. Obviously, I would have done it if I had to.

So off he went with the firing squad and did his job. Of course the officers, if the people weren't killed, had to finish them off with the revolver. He came back looking pretty awful – all of them [did]. And this officer went into his billet and stayed inside. Some kind person had put a whisky bottle and a cup inside. The next morning the bottle had been emptied. Frightful for him. I was ashamed of myself, but I couldn't. I know my limitations.

Later this officer wasn't the same and we took this hill. He was in my Company and I kept well down the other side of the hill, so I wasn't too conspicuous. This officer kept walking along the top of the hill asking in my opinion to be killed. Frightful, and he was.

It's the only thing I look back on in my military career with shame.[10]

A gunner of the Tank Corps describes what he witnessed:

I witnessed a shooting at P——— prison. It was a young boy, far under age. All he needed was his birth certificate. But he was found crying in a shell hole and that was it. They dug a hole, filled it with water and put in a pole, which soon froze solid. Then he was marched out. A PH gas helmet was put over his head backwards and he was tied to the post. Then ten of his very own platoon were ordered to fire, one round being blank. But the APM stood over him with his revolver, just in case they missed. Afterwards they all said they never aimed at him.

It shook me a bit, as at that time they had not got the

confirmation from England that my story was true, as up to that time I was under suspicion of being a spy and treated accordingly.[11]

Medical officers also had a role to play, as highlighted by a major who had qualified as a doctor in 1917:

The night before I went into his little cell which was simply covered with straw and I couldn't tell him what was going to happen the next day. I gave him a quarter of a grain of morphine. I don't remember if it was an ambulance or what it was, but I was taken to Poperinghe Military Prison. I found the man sat in a chair in front of a firing squad. I had to go up and pin a piece of paper from my note book. The officer gave the command for fire. The firing was wild, very wild and I went up to make sure that he was dead. Had he not been, the officer with his loaded revolver had to do the necessary execution. But it was not required.

To my mind he was fairly self-composed. I would put him down as a brave man.[12]

A medical officer in France took a somewhat harder view regarding shell-shock and execution:

A fellow came running in and he was a well known shell-shocker, he had done it before. An officer threw himself on the floor and said 'Oh! I'm shell-shocked, I'm shell-shocked,' and went into sort of spasms. He was just a frightened man. In the Second World War that came to be recognized as shell-shock, but in the First World War that was just fear. But I never reported that to anybody; of course I just sent him back.

I remember a fellow joining us who'd been very heavily shot over at Mons. He joined us in the later stage of the war, and the first time we went out on a route march, we had to move from one place to another. Every time we heard a shell, we took no notice of it, we were so used to them coming near us or hitting us. He threw himself on the floor, you know, lay down until it all passed. That was a case of shock. He'd been in so much of that and seen so many killed by it that he expected every shell came to kill him.

When we were having a fortnight's rest, out of the line, which was a habit when one was occupying the trenches – you had a fortnight in the front and a fortnight in the village – the Colonel sent for me and said, 'I have a very unpleasant duty for you which I won't like any more than you do.' And then he told me what it was all about. Apparently one of our men had absented himself from the front line on two occasions when a battle had started, and after the battle was over he came back and made some excuse that he'd mislaid the way. . . . The court martial sentenced him to death by firing squad, and the unpleasant task the Colonel set me was to attend the shooting and to pin on his heart a piece of coloured flannel – so as to give the marksmen something to fire at.

The following morning he was to be shot at dawn. I lay awake thinking of it all night and I thought, well I'll try to help this fellow a bit. So I took down a cupful of brandy and presented it to him and said, 'Drink this and you won't know very much about it.' He said, 'What is it?' I said, 'It's brandy.' He said, 'Well I've never drunk spirits in my life, there's no point in my starting now.' That was a sort of spurious sort of courage in a way. Two men came and led him out of the hut where he had been guarded all night. As he left the hut his legs gave way. Then one could see fear entering his heart. Rather than march to the firing spot, he was dragged along. When he got there he had his hands tied behind his back. He was put up against a wall, his eyes were bandaged and the firing squad were given the order to fire.

The firing squad consisted of eight men, only two of whom had their rifles loaded [with live rounds]. The other six carried blank ammunition. That was so that they wouldn't actually know who had fired the fatal shot. I wondered at the time, what on earth will happen if they miss him and they don't kill him completely? I was very anxious about that. But, when they fired, he fell to the ground, writhing as all people do, even if they have been killed – they have this reflex action, which goes on for some minutes. I didn't know whether he was dead or not, but at that moment the sergeant in charge stepped forward, put a revolver to his head and blew his brains out, and that was the coup de grace. Which I learnt afterwards was always carried out in these cases of shooting.

This medical officer was asked the following questions: 'This was obviously a very radical punishment for a man whose crime was what perhaps today might be regarded as a nervous illness. As a medical man, at the time did you think this sentence and this penalty was a reasonable one?' He replied:

I think it was absolutely essential. It was setting a bad example to the men. They would begin to feel that you only had to walk off during a battle and then come back afterwards and you escaped any penalty of death or mutilation. It was setting a bad example. It must have happened, I dare say, in the Second World War, [but] it didn't happen so much. They were looked on as shell-shocked cases instead of being just as they were, cowards, and I think it was a necessary punishment.

I think they were rather softer, yes.[13]

References

1. Public Record Office, Kew, ref. WO 93/49: tabular statement.
2. Public Record Office, Kew, ref. WO 93/49: Paper 71.
3. Public Record Office, Kew, ref. WO 93/49: Paper 73.
4. Public Record Office, Kew, ref. WO 93/49: Memorandum on the difference between military offences of Cowardice and Desertion.

5. Public Record Office, Kew, ref. WO 93/49: Reference 52.
6. Public Record Office, Kew, ref. WO 93/49: Papers 74 and 78.
7. BBC Radio 4, 7.20pm, Thursday 16 September, 1993: 'Document' by Julian Putkowski.
8. Imperial War Museum, Department of Documents: Canon T.G. Rogers, 2nd Guards Brigade, Guards Division, Letter: 31 May, 1916.
9. Liddle Collection, University of Leeds: The Rev. Noel Mellish VC MC KKC, Hon. Chaplain to the Royal Fusiliers, Reference 11, General Section, execution.
10. Imperial War Museum, Department of Sound Records: Eric Wolton, ref. SR 9090/11.
11. Liddle Collection, University of Leeds: G.B. Mason, Reference 7, General Section, execution.
12. Liddle Collection, University of Leeds: Major F. Gamm, Tape 654, 31 May, 1982.
13. Imperial War Museum, Department of Sound Records: Captain M.S. Esler, Reel 2, ref. 378-03.

CHAPTER SIX

Shot at Dawn

Once Field Marshal Haig had confirmed sentence, matters proceeded at some speed.

> General Officer Commanding
> Fifth Army
> In confirmation of my telegram No A [b] 2110 of today. Please note that the C in C has confirmed the sentence in the case of Temp. Sub-Lieutenant E.L.A. Dyett RNVR of the Nelson Battalion, 63rd Division.
>
> It should be noted that under the Army Act an officer does not cease to be an officer by reason of sentence of death being promulgated. Sub-Lieutenant Dyett should therefore not be deprived of his badge of rank before the sentence is carried out.
>
> Please return the proceedings to this office after promulgation.
> 2/1/1917   AAG for Adjutant General
>   HQ 63rd RN Division
> Officer Commanding
> 'Nelson' Battalion

> Forwarded. The attached proceedings are to be promulgated to Sub-Lieutenant E.L.A. Dyett, by an experienced officer of your Battalion, after which these proceedings are to be handed to the APM.
>
> Instructions as to how this promulgation is to be done will be given direct to you by the APM.

The APM is authorized to issue to you all future instructions in this case, and you will ensure that these are implicitly carried out.

On no account are these proceedings to be promulgated or made public to your Battalion or to any unnecessary persons until you receive further instructions.

R.D.H. Lough
Major DAA & QMC
63rd RN Division[1]

3rd January 1917

Edwin Dyett was playing cards with two Battalion officers when another officer opened the big blue envelope and read out his Death Warrant – he was to be shot at dawn. A Padre was standing by and spent an hour with him so he could make his peace with God. He had the strength to write one last letter home, which is as follows:

France January 4, 1917

Dearest Mother Mine, I hope by now you will have had the news. Dearest, I am leaving you now because He has willed it. My sorrow tonight is for the trouble I have caused you and dad.

Please excuse any mistakes, but if it were not for the kind support of the Rev. W.C. —— who is with me tonight, I should not be able to write myself. I should like you to write to him, as he has been my friend.

I am leaving all my effects to you, dearest; will you give my little —— half the sum you have of mine?

Give dear Dad my love and wish him luck. I feel for you so much and I am sorry for bringing dishonour upon you all. Give —— my love. She will, I expect, understand – and give her back the presents, photos, cards, etc., she has sent me, poor girl.

So now dearest Mother, I must close. May God bless and protect you all now and for evermore. Amen.[2]

Now there was nothing for it but to wait and think, through the cold winter's night. Think of what he had known, who he had known and what he would deeply miss. It must have been all the harder knowing that he was not a criminal or indeed a murderer, just a person who had failed to come up to expectations. Part of a poem by another Royal Naval Division officer, Rupert Brooke, called 'The Great Lover', highlights what a man would miss in this world:

These I have loved:
    White plates and cups, clean-gleaming,
Ringed with blue lines; and feathery, faery dust;
Wet roofs, beneath the lamp light; the strong crust
Of friendly bread; and many-tasting food;
Rainbows; and the blue bitter smoke of wood;
And radiant raindrops couching in cool flowers;
And flowers themselves, that sway through sunny hours,
Dreaming of moths that drink them under the moon;
Then, the cool kindliness of sheets, that soon
Smooth away trouble; and the rough male kiss
Of blankets; grainy wood; live hair that is
Shining and free; blue-massing clouds; the keen
Unpassioned beauty of a great machine;
The benison of hot water; furs to touch;
The good smell of old clothes; and other such–
The comfortable smell of friendly fingers,
Hair's fragrance, and the must reek that lingers
About dead leaves and last year's ferns . . .
                                        Dear names,
And thousand other throng to me! Royal flames;
Sweet water's dimpling laugh from tap or spring;
Holes in the ground; and voices that do sing;
Voices in laughter, too; and body's pain,
Soon turned to peace; and the deep-panting train;
Firm sands; the little dulling edge of foam
That browns and dwindles as the wave goes home;
And washen stones, gay for an hour; the cold
Graveness of iron; moist black earthen mould;
Sleep; and high places; footprints in the dew;
And oaks; and brown horse-chestnuts, glossy-new;
And new-peeled sticks; and shining pools on grass–
All these have been my loves. And these shall pass[3]

And so with the coming of dawn Dyett had to face his death. The 23 February, 1918 issue of the newspaper *John Bull* which had an eye witness present, describes what happened:

> Can you picture that final scene? The prisoner tied to a stake; there was no need – he faced death fearlessly, but the cords cut him and he protested – his eyes bandaged, his identification disc suspended just over his left breast. The firing party, half-hidden in a trench. No time is wasted. And yet there comes the cry: 'For God's sake put me out of my misery – this suspense is killing me'. And, as the rifles make their first click, 'Well, boys, good-bye! For God's sake, shoot straight.' And this from one who stood there and saw it all: 'He was no coward; he behaved like a pukka white man'. And this from the lad himself, in that dread hour: 'Yes I can face this, but I couldn't face the Boche.'[4]

J. Blacklock of the Nelson Battalion stated:

> I got off it, got out of being on the firing squad. I said to the Petty Officer, 'I will never sleep well if I shot one of our own'.

Referring to Dyett, Blacklock said: 'He told them to shoot straight, that's what he said!'[5]

The Padre wrote:

> I enclose your boy's last letter to his mother. I want you to understand he wrote it entirely by himself, his mind being as clear and thoughtful as anyone could wish; not a tremor or moment of fear. When his end had been carried out [by order of GCM], I accompanied his body in an ambulance car several miles away to a beautiful little cemetery, near a small town, quite close to the sea, and here we buried him with the Church of England Service. A cross will soon be erected over his grave. Leave it to me, and I will see that it is done, before our hurried departure to another part of France.[6]

Dyett's death warrant was endorsed by the APM, Lieutenant (Temporary Captain) Royal Marines C.T.J.G. Walmesley, formerly of the Berkshire Yeomanry with the words:

> Sentence duly carried out at St: Firmin at 7.30am on Friday Jany, 5th 1917.

The words are just scrawled across the page, in a careless manner. It's as if the writer was shocked. He made a mistake with the date, starting to put Thursday, but stopped halfway through, crossing out his error and initialling it.

There is nothing more apart from an endorsement by Herbert J. Davidson RAMC, attached to 2nd Field Artillery, 63rd (RN) Division, with the words: 'Death was instantaneous'.[7]

Ernest Thurtle, Member of Parliament and campaigner against the execution of servicemen, in his book *Military Discipline and Democracy*, writes the following:

> In July 1919 a gallant infantry officer, Colonel Lambert Ward, appealed in the House of Commons against any differentiation between the graves of those who had been killed in action, or had died of wounds or sickness, and those unfortunate men who had been shot for cowardice or desertion. In the midst of a painful silence that could be felt he spoke as follows:
>
>> I ask the House not to dismiss this petition with the remark that these men were cowards and deserved their fate. They were not cowards in the accepted meaning of the word. At any rate they did not display one-tenth part of the cowardice that was displayed by the crowds in London who went flocking to the Tube Stations on the first alarm of an air raid. These men, many of them, volunteered in the early days of the war to serve their country. They tried and they failed . . .

> I think that it is well that it should be made pub-
> licly known and that the people of this country
> should understand . . . that from the point of view
> of Tommy up in the trenches, war is not a question
> of honours and decorations, but war is just hell . . .

Thurtle continues: 'In uttering these words, the soldier
was lifting a corner of the veil of make-believe which hides
from the public the real feelings of the actual fighting men
of an army.'[8]

In April, 1922, the Imperial War Graves Commission
wrote to the Judge Advocate General at the War Office asking to be furnished with a list of soldiers who were
sentenced and executed by field general court martial
during the war. This was done, as the Commission had
decided on consideration to erect headstones of the usual
pattern over the graves without reference to the manner of
death. Today such graves are marked by standard
Commonwealth War Graves Commission headstones, and
the names appear in their registers in the same way as other
casualties. These graves are maintained to the same standard and they are awarded equal treatment with other
graves in their care.[9]

But what of the Nelson Battalion? How did they remember their brother officer? They didn't. On 26 December
Dyett's court martial is mentioned, but in the entry for 5
January, 1917, nothing appears. Just 'brigade practice
attack, Vercourt'. It's as if he had never existed, his memory wiped away.[10]

Thomas MacMillan, the clerk to 189th Brigade, wrote
later:

> Without going out of my way I learned that the unfor-
> tunate officer had waited so long for the verdict to be
> promulgated that he and his guard held the strong belief
> that he would be given a chance to redeem himself. He
> was actually playing cards with two officers when the
> fatal news was communicated to him and he was given
> only a few hours to prepare for death.

Some days after the shooting a bulky package arrived at Brigade Headquarters and I found it contained all the papers bearing on the trial. I had only time to glance over them when I was summoned to the mess, and I had no option but to take the papers with me. That was the last I saw of them, but my hasty perusal sufficed to disclose who the witnesses for the prosecution were, and from that moment I resolved to shun them both, for one of them was none other than the Petty Officer who shaped so badly on the Peninsula and the other an officer for whom I had a very poor regard.

I had also observed that, although the young officer had been found Guilty, there was a strong recommendation to mercy, and in common with others I wondered what consideration had been given to the recommendation.

Was he, I wondered, to be the first martyr to the clamour from the ranks for an example to be made of an officer for desertion or cowardice? How is it, the men were asking and rightly so, that only rankers are being shot for cowardice? How many officers have been guilty of this offence and why have they not been made to answer for it with their lives, as we have to do? The higher Command must have heard this grouse grow louder and could not fail to admit the justice of it.

If, however, they were forced to act, why did they select a mere boy for their first victim? It was obvious that the lad had been commissioned to control men before he had learned to control himself. Surely there were senior officers who had been guilty of desertion or cowardice – officers whose age, experience and responsibility made their crime so much more reprehensible.

The unfortunate youth had been well represented at his trial by a fellow officer who was a qualified solicitor. As there was a fair proportion of men with legal training in fighting units, some horrible individual, far removed from the danger zone, conceived the sinister plan of withdrawing all such and attaching them to the

Judge Advocate's department, and soon this was given effect to.

Many left to join the circus, but this officer who acted as Prisoner's Friend in the case in question carried on with his soldiering and, if he had not all his wits about him, he might have paid dearly for the part he played at the trial.

This last comment is very illuminating as to the attitude of the senior officers at that time. MacMillan wrote about this also, when making up lists of officers before the Division's action at Gavrelle:

The Battalion had been instructed to render a statement giving names of the officers who would participate in the next fight and, as the lists arrived, I took them to the Major. His eagle eye observed that the officer who had acted as Prisoner's Friend to the young man who was 'Shot at Dawn' was on the reserve list. At this his monkey rose, and in his most unbearing manner he told me to instruct the Battalion Commander concerned to send the 'hard-faced bastard forward'. But the young gent thus referred to knew all the tricks of his trade. On being informed of Brigade's intentions concerning him, he promptly developed a raging temperature and as promptly was evacuated to England![11]

References

1. Public Record Office, Kew, ref. ADM/156/24.
2. *John Bull*, 23 February, 1918.
3. *The Complete Poems of Rupert Brooke*, Sidgwick & Jackson, 1918.
4. *John Bull*, 23 February, 1918.
5. Liddle Collection, Leeds University: J. Blacklock, Nelson Battalion, RND, Tape 76, June, 1971.
6. *John Bull*, 23 February 1918.

7. Public Record Office, Kew, ref. ADM/156/24.
8. Thurtle, Ernest, *Military Discipline and Democracy*, C.W. Daniel, 1920.
9. Commonwealth War Graves Commission letter to L.G. Sellers of 11 November 1991.
10. Public Record Office, Kew, ref. ADM 137/3065; Nelson Battalion War Diary.
11. Imperial War Museum, Department of Documents: Thomas MacMillan.

13. Battle of the Ancre; ruins of the railway station, November, 1916.

14. An improvised bridge across the Ancre, November, 1916.

15. Water refilling point on the Ancre by the Hamel — St Pierre
Divion road.

16. Roadside field kitchen near Hamel.

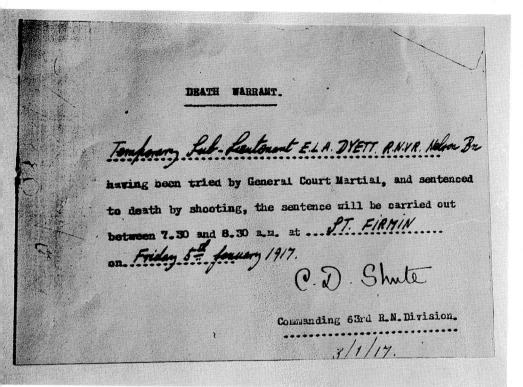

DEATH WARRANT.

Temporary Sub-Lieutenant E.L.A. DYETT R.N.V.R. Nelson Bn
having been tried by General Court Martial, and sentenced
to death by shooting, the sentence will be carried out
between 7.30 and 8.30 a.m. at ...*ST. FIRMIN*.....
on...*Friday 5th January 1917.*

C. D. Shute

Commanding 63rd R.N. Division.
....

3/1/17.

17. Dyett's death warrant…

18. …Confirmed by the Commander-in-Chief.

Confirmed

D. Haig . F.M.

2 Jany 17

19. Dyett's grave at Le Crotoy cemetery.

20. The covers of *John Bull* magazine, 23 February and 16 March, 1918.

CHAPTER SEVEN

A Hornets' Nest

Like a bolt from the blue, news of Dyett's death reached his father, Commander W.H.R. Dyett, in early 1917. Stupefaction, indignation and finally wrath set in. So began a campaign by his father to clear his son's name. After requests by the writer and extensive enquiries by departments of the Ministry of Defence, no trace of any correspondence can be found. The Ministry destroy a great deal of material in the process of deciding what should be kept for the historian. However, by 1919 Commander Dyett informed his family that Edwin had been vindicated. What this exoneration was is not known; there is nothing on the court-martial file to suggest a later pardon. In Julian Putkowski and Julian Sykes's book published in 1989 appears information that Dyett had been awarded the Victory and Defence Medals for his services in the First World War.[1] From my own enquiries and researches at the Public Record Office at Kew, I could find no record of this. But a detestation and loathing of the system had taken hold of the Commander; he left Britain, with his family, for a fresh start in the New World, never to return, and gave up his British citizenship.

On 23 February, 1918, Horatio Bottomley in his paper *John Bull* published an article entitled 'Shot at Dawn: A Trench Tragedy – Plea For The Officer – Court Martial Reform'. In it he outlined the facts, as known, concerning the execution of Edwin Dyett. The story caused a stir in both the public and in Parliament. Some of the points he raised are outlined below:

And now comes the tragedy. On Boxing Day this boy officer was summoned before a Court Martial to be tried for his life. That in itself is sad enough in all conscience, but what is to be said when I tell you that he did not see the officer who was to defend him until half-an-hour before the trial? And yet between the day of his offence and the hour of trial, no less than six weeks had elapsed. This may or may not be in accordance with the usual procedure, but it seems to me, as a layman, that during the whole preliminary inquiry into any serious charge against an officer he should be afforded the fullest opportunity of legal assistance. Such a right is conceded in civil life to the meanest criminal. That is my first indictment of a system which, in the interests of justice and humanity, must be reformed – and at once. It is conceivable that if an accused soldier's case was properly conducted at the preliminary stage, it might not pass to the point of a Court Martial. But bad as is the existing practice – it is a travesty to say, as does the *Manual of Military Law*, that the procedure is on all fours with that of our British Courts of Justice – it becomes criminal when we reflect what happened in this case. The officer who defended may have been the finest advocate at the Bar. But I say, solemnly, that it was an outrage to expect that man to play the part of the 'Soldier's Friend' almost at a moment's notice. I challenge denial of the statement that Counsel did not see the prisoner – a lad on trial for his life – until half-an-hour before the court opened. And what of the Court? It was composed of officers, from a Brigadier-General downwards, all superior in rank to the Sub-Lieutenant whose fate rested in their hands. Is this trial by one's peers? Read this: 'In trials before Courts Martial the members of the courts both find the facts and lay down the law, and thus perform the functions of both judge and jury. It therefore becomes their duty, when applying their minds to questions of fact in the capacity of jury-men, to consider themselves bound by the rules which in the case of an ordinary trial are laid down by the judge.' And that is what is expected of officers who may be, and generally are, entirely ignorant of the law. It is true a Deputy Judge Advocate assists them, but it is they who are called upon to play the dual role of judge and jury. That in this case they did not do their level and honest best I am not going to suggest for an instant. But considering that the principal witness was an officer whom the accused described as his 'one and only enemy', I ask what opportunity had the defending officer of eliciting evidence as to credibility and antecedents when he was pitchforked into the trial at the last moment? The grossest criminal who ever lived would, under the protecting wing of British Justice, have had a fairer run for life – that I say with the utmost deliberation. You see, although there is a court of Criminal Appeal for a foul murderer – Voisin, who killed and cut up a French woman, has just had his chance in our courts – there is none for an Officer or Private. 'There is not, in the ordinary sense of the word,' says the *Manual* already quoted, 'any appeal from the decision of a Court Martial.'[2]

On 20 February, 1918, Philip Morrell MP, the Liberal Member for Burnley, raised the subject of courts martial and execution of soldiers during a debate on Army estimates:

I now come to the difficult question of trials by court martial and military executions. What is called the death penalty is at the very root of military discipline. You cannot carry on the Army in the stern business of war, or keep discipline in that vast organization, without the death penalty. At the same time, it is a very simple question, because it must appeal to all our humanity. The stories that come to one of these death penalties and sentences are most poignant. Of all the horrors of war, I

think nothing is more horrible than that men are condemned to be shot, and are actually shot by their
comrades, in many cases for failure of nerves, or it may
be sleeping at their posts – as something which does not
necessarily show moral delinquency, but only grave
neglect of duty. It is a stern, a terribly stern, necessity
that this should be so; but we are bound to see that the
conditions under which these trials take place are as fair
as possible. We are bound to ask questions, and to bring
before the House any case which we think demands
investigation. There is necessarily a considerable amount
of obscurity with regard to this question. There is obscurity because we do not know the number. It is
contrary to the public interests, we are told, to disclose
the facts. There is also obscurity because the evidence of
the minutes of the court martial cannot be known; so
that it is very difficult for the relations to inquire into
what has happened in a case where one of these executions has taken place. So for that reason there is great
uncertainty, which makes the subject all the more difficult. It will be wrong, and it will be foolish, to blind our
eyes to the fact that there is a great, widespread, and
deep public interest with regard to this subject.

Mr Morrell then produced a copy of the week's *John Bull*
containing the article on Edwin Dyett:

> This article will be read by many thousands of people
> up and down the country, and therefore there is no need
> to keep it secret, because it is published, and it will be
> read. It gives the details of the trial and execution of this
> young officer. [Morrell then outlined the circumstances
> of the case, and continued:] What I would say I felt was
> that it is no doubt substantially true, and if not true then
> the editor of the paper ought to be prosecuted. If it is
> true, I think it goes to show, like many other facts which
> have come to my knowledge, that there is a case for
> investigation as to the method of procedure in these
> courts martial. I don't say more.

Where a man has been wounded and suffers from shell-shock there ought to be special care taken and special Regulations dealing with such cases. If a man has once suffered from shell-shock he is liable to fail again. I do not say that care is not taken, but I think these cases ought to be treated separately, and that the Regulations ought to be altered. It is possible there may be special Regulations on the subject, and I think there ought to be. For instance, in such a case where shell-shock is alleged there ought always to be possible revision or a chance of appeal. There should be a second chance or something of that sort, or at any rate some special Regulations putting those cases apart from other cases. The second point upon which I hope my hon. Friend will be able to give some assurance is the question of the 'prisoner's friend'. That case has been raised again and again by question in this House, and only lately by me when I asked that in no case should a man be put on trial for his life without having the opportunity of a proper defence from an expert advisor, and, when he cannot get legal advice in France, that he should have an expert advisor as 'prisoner's friend'.

The allegation is made by my hon. Friend the member for Blackburn [Mr Snowden] that out of twenty-five cases of execution which occurred in October last, twenty-four of the men had no 'prisoner's friend' to conduct their defence, and that in only one case was the man properly defended, while twenty-four stood alone before the court martial. I suggest that the man should always have a 'prisoner's friend' without asking for him, unless he actually refused his help. I believe that is a practice in civil cases, and that a judge will never consent to try a man for his life without seeing that the man has the benefit of counsel to defend him.

The third reform which I desire to see is that there should be a chance of revision in these cases by a competent legal tribunal. There is at present, I know, a revision of the case by the Judge Advocate General. I do not think that is enough, and that there ought to be the same chance of a trial by a Court of Appeal as a man has in civil life.[3]

The Under-Secretary of State for War, Ian Macpherson, in his reply said:

> He has quoted a specific case of an officer who has suffered the death penalty *in very extraordinary circumstances*. If the Committee would allow me, I should like, before I express any opinion upon it, to have all the facts investigated, because one finds very often that those cases – not from any unpatriotic spirit – are dealt with in a way which often leave a good deal of room for doubt in the minds of ordinary men.[4]

On 2 March, 1918, the newspaper *John Bull* produced a second article, which was most probably by Horatio Bottomley himself. I reproduce this below, in order to help the reader appreciate the interest that was being generated at the time:

'Shot At Dawn'
Further Amazing Revelations – A Callous Act

> Our story of the young officer of the Royal Naval Division who was tried and shot in circumstances, which in our opinion have cast the gravest suspicion on Court-Martial methods, has evoked the greatest public interest. In telling that story, with such information as was at our disposal, we were scrupulously careful not to overstate anything in favour of the accused. But now that the case has been raised in the House of Commons, and the Under-Secretary for War has promised to 'see the proceedings', and, 'consistently with his duty, and with the law, explain to the House the real facts of the case', we propose to throw some further light on the criminal callousness of the methods employed. And here

let us say that a mere examination of the 'proceedings' will not satisfy us – the whole of the circumstance preliminary to and after the trial should form the subject of a special inquiry. Assuming, as we naturally did, that, in spite of the disgraceful insufficiency of the time allowed the 'prisoner's friend' to study the case, the ordinary procedure was followed when the verdict had been arrived at, we wrote: 'The boy knew of the sentence of death, but he also knew of the recommendation to mercy'.

A Terrible Awakening

If our later information is correct – and we have good reason for trusting the source – he had not the faintest idea that he had been found guilty, even with a recommendation to mercy, until 7.45pm the night prior to his execution, when an officer stepped into the room and read the warrant. Here is a young fellow with the shadow of death hanging over him for days, and he pitifully ignorant of his awful fate. He was allowed to live on in the belief that the worst that could befall him was the loss of his commission. We repeat, the foulest murderer who ever did to death an innocent victim is given the right of appeal: and, that appeal failing, is allowed such interval of time as Christian humanity can suggest before he passes from this world into the Unknown. Not so this young officer. Barely twelve hours between learning his fate and facing the firing party! And here is another point – which no examination of the 'proceedings' will reveal to the Under-Secretary for War. We understand the Prisoner's Friend did see his 'client' before that meeting half an hour in advance of the trial, but in what circumstances? He saw him in his billet on Christmas Day – the trial was on Boxing Day – but at that time he did not possess the Summary of Evidence, nor was the accused able to tell the exact charge on which he was to be arraigned the next day. It was not until half an hour before the Court Martial opened that the defending counsel was handed the Summary of Evidence – that was taken at the preliminary hearings when the accused was undefended – and not until he actually entered the court did the Deputy Judge Advocate General hand him the Charge Sheet which revealed the alternative charge of conduct subversive of good order and military discipline.

A Doubtful 'Order'

There is a further matter to which the Under-Secretary for War should direct his attention, when he seeks to discover why these recommendations to mercy were ignored, and who was responsible for their being ignored. We believe a strong point was made at the trial that the junior officer – 'my one and only enemy', as the lad wrote to his mother – who gave him orders, was not a company officer. He was attached to HQ as a Dump Officer, and wore a pale blue band round his sleeve. His duty for the day was merely to replenish the various ammunition dumps and he had no authority whatever to issue orders to company officers. That was why the lad desired to return to Brigade HQ for confirmation of this junior's orders. We repeat that the unvarnished tale we have felt it our duty to tell is one that must demand something more than the War Office examination of the 'papers' in the case. Already our revelations have led to the issue of a definite Army Order to all COs, laying down what is the proper procedure at Courts Martial, and emphasizing the rules of justice which must be observed. We cannot bring back to life this young lad, who in our view was sacrificed, if not wantonly, then with a shocking disregard for just and humane methods. But we can insist that the whole system of Courts Martial shall be drastically revised so that the soldier shall at least find as much protection in law as the civilian.[5]

It was not until 6 March, 1918, that Philip Morrell MP asked the Under-Secretary of State for War if he had made inquiries into the case which was recently brought to his notice of a young officer who was condemned to death and shot on or about 27 December, although recommended to mercy by the court; and had he any further statement to make upon the case?

Mr Macpherson replied:

> I have made enquiries into the case mentioned, and I find that the recommendation to mercy was duly considered by the various and many authorities through whom the court-martial proceedings passed before submission to the Field Marshal Commanding-in-Chief for confirmation. I am advised that the proceedings are entirely in order. I have, therefore, no further statement to make upon the case.

Mr Morrell's rejoinder was, 'Do I understand the facts as published are substantially correct?' To which Macpherson replied, 'No; my hon. Friend must not understand that.' Morrell went on by asking the Under-Secretary of State for War if the Government would consider the advisability of providing the right of appeal in special cases. This was turned down. Undaunted, Morrell requested that regulations be provided so that no soldier should be tried before a General Court Martial, on a capital charge, without the assistance of a 'prisoner's friend'.

Macpherson's reply was:

> A soldier tried by General or District Court Martial on any charge has already, under Rules of Procedure 87–94, the right to be assisted by a friend or to be represented by counsel. At Field General Courts Martial an accused is always, in practice, allowed to be so assisted or represented whenever possible, though this is not expressly provided by the Rules in the case of such courts. If an accused on a capital charge before any court martial, desires to be represented, and finds a

difficulty in securing a friend or counsel, a suitable officer would be found for the purpose whenever possible.
The Army Council have recently issued a reaffirming
order on this subject.

Mr Pemberton Billing MP asked: 'Is it not possible to
arrange that a man shall have a friend with him before the
court martial?' Macpherson replied, 'In practice that has
been done during the war; the man has always had a friend.'
Morrell said, 'Could not my hon. Friend get the Regulations
so altered as to make what is the usual practice the invariable rule?' The Under-Secretary replied, 'As a matter of fact,
in this war it has been the invariable rule.' Mr Outhwaite
asked, 'What happens when a suitable officer, engaged by
the parents of the man, can be present, and what happens
if it is not possible to find a suitable officer?' Macpherson
said, 'In all the cases that I have investigated – and I have
investigated a great many – a suitable officer has been found
in every case. In the Navy and Army there are numbers of
young barristers and solicitors who would be only too will-
ing to come forward.' Major Davis then said, 'Is there any
reason why these officers cannot be appointed in order to
see that this work is carried out by the responsible officers
who are doing it?' The Under-Secretary replied, 'I cannot
accept that statement. My belief is that this work is carried
out thoroughly and conscientiously.'[6]
So the official line was one of complacency. We know
that a great number of men who were tried for their lives
did not have a prisoner's friend. No doubt, if requested, one
would be found, but a nervous young man, not fully aware
of his entitlement rather than his right in law, would not
push for this representation, but would go, naked and
alone, before his accusers. Macpherson might well have
investigated a number of cases, but his selection has to be
called into question.
John Bull was to fire another broadside in its issue of 16
March, 1918. Once again I reproduce the substance of the
article as it is very important to the story.

LET THEM PROSECUTE ME!

Another Rex v. Bottomley? – The Case For The War Office – I adhere to My Charges

As I hinted last week, the Government have had under consideration the question of prosecuting this journal in respect of its recent articles 'Shot At Dawn' – which have caused such deep interest throughout the country, and also at the Front. I treated the threat with some indifference – knowing full well that, whatever other blunders the authorities may commit, they are not likely to embark upon a step which would set the whole Army by the ears, quite apart from the fact that I think I know my rights as well as my responsibilities as a public journalist. Whether they have since thought better of the idea – or, as is more probable, have been advised not to make so false a move – I cannot say. But they are now apparently in saner mood, as will be gathered from the following correspondence:

War Office, Whitehall, SW1

Dear Mr Bottomley,

The two articles in *John Bull* which recently appeared, entitled 'Shot at Dawn', have attracted the attention of the Secretary of State, and he desires me to say that as the articles are based on misapprehensions of fact he takes the first opportunity of informing you that, if you will make an appointment with the Director of Personnel Services at the War Office, that officer will be prepared to show you all the true facts of the case.

I might add that your articles are full of inaccuracies, which I feel sure you would desire to have corrected, and I also feel sure that when you criticize you would prefer to criticize upon the facts as established rather than upon suppositions which have doubtless been conveyed to you by persons who have trusted to their memory.

Yours faithfully,
R.W. Brade

Sir Reginald Brade, War Office, Whitehall, SW1

Dear Sir Reginald,

I am obliged for your letter of the 1st inst., and greatly appreciate the courtesy of your offer to allow me an opportunity of making myself further acquainted with the facts of the painful case dealt with in our recent articles, 'Shot At Dawn'. I assure you, however, that before publishing these articles, every possible step was taken by us to ascertain the real facts; and I need scarcely say that if in any material respect we have been misled we shall be only too happy to do whatever is right. I am bound, however, to add that I shall want a lot of convincing that we have gone farther than the circumstances justify.

If convenient to you, I will call upon the Director of Personnel Services on Friday afternoon next, at 3.30, and perhaps you would allow me to bring with me my Assistant Editor, Mr Charles Palmer, who has given very special attention to this matter.

Yours faithfully,
Horatio Bottomley

And, accordingly, to the Director of Personnel Services at the War Office we duly repaired, remaining there for upwards of two hours – listening to a most amazing series of official explanations and 'corrections' and expositions of military and civil law – with which I shall deal in a moment. Let me say at once, however, that the interview has left me more convinced than ever of the justice of our charges against the present system, under which boy officers are sometimes done to death without any fair chance of defence – whilst, even in such cases, there is at present no appeal of any kind. Indeed from beginning to end of his trial, the nerve-shaken young officer, under arrest, is in a worse position than the burglar at Bow Street and the Old Bailey. So far from withdrawing my allegations, or offering any apology for them, I decline to modify them in any substantial particular.

The Case and the Reply

Let me restate the charges I have brought, not so much against the administration as against the system of Courts Martial in general, and as applied to this young officer in particular. When a soldier is placed under arrest, he is denied the right of any legal assistance during the preliminary investigation, being permitted simply to attend in person and question the witnesses. Imagine a young private or a boy officer, whose very offence may be due to nerve shock, appearing, in person, before his superior officers in the role of cross-examiner! Why, even a man charged with murder is in a better position. Well, what was the official answer to this charge? Absolutely none. 'It is the law, as laid down in the *Manual of Military Law*.' As the gravedigger [sic] in Hamlet put it, it is 'crowner's quest law'; and that settles it. Then as to the second charge. It is that when the preliminary inquiry is finished and the accused is arraigned for trial by Court Martial, no adequate opportunity is given for the preparation of his defence – even when, as in the case of this young officer, the charge is one involving the death sentence. I will assume that the boy was duly furnished with the copy of the Charge Sheet and Summary of Evidence – but what he did with them there is no means of ascertaining. All we do know is that the officer who was ordered, literally at the eleventh hour, to defend him, applied for the Summary so soon as he knew that he had to act as 'Prisoner's Friend', and that he did not receive it until half-an-hour before the trial. This, I repeat, was a scandalous proceeding. Even if he had received the evidence twenty-four hours before the court sat, that in my view would have been a wholly inadequate time in which to prepare the defence. There was no opportunity of obtaining evidence as to the character of the witnesses who were to testify against this lad, and in this particular case that matter was of importance, for, as I have already shown, the unhappy youth declared that all the trouble arose at the instance of his 'one and only enemy' – as to whom there were circumstances which were never, I believe, brought to the knowledge of the Court. But, when I put this point to the Director of Personnel Services, I again receive the answer: 'It is the law'. The official mind is apparently quite incapable of realizing the situation in which a boy, suddenly confronted with the ordeal of trial for his life – overwrought and unstrung and without any previous conference with or help from any legal adviser – is suddenly called upon personally to instruct his own counsel – or, rather, the counsel who, a complete stranger and conceivably quite ignorant of military law, is put up to defend him as best he can. So overwrought was this poor boy that, as we have seen, he never gave his papers to his Counsel who was left to find out the actual facts for himself: and who, even had he in view of these circumstances asked for a postponement of the trial, could not, according to these precious Regulations, have secured an interval of grace of more than a few hours!

Another Rex v. Bottomley

So far, I think it will be conceded that nothing very terrible in the shape of 'misapprehensions of fact' or 'inaccuracies' had been revealed at this War Office interview. And up to this point, at any rate, I felt quite safe from arrest, under any section of the all-accommodating DORA [Defence of the Realm Act]. But it was with feelings of some trepidation that I approached the presentation of 'all the true facts of the case', so kindly promised by Sir Reginald Brade. Here, thought I, will come the case for the Crown in another Rex v. Bottomley. For I had not failed to notice that the dossier of the full proceedings of the Court Martial was lying in front of me on the table. On the top of the bundle was the Charge Sheet, and that was the first document to be quoted against me. With an air of great authority, I was assured that I had most inaccurately stated the charge against the officer, as being that of desertion in the face of the enemy, 'In that he failed to join his Battalion in the line when ordered to do so.' That was quite wrong, I was told. The real charge was that 'when it was his duty to join his Battalion which was engaged in operations against the enemy, he did not do so.' Now, I am supposed to be a bit of a lawyer, but for the life of me I couldn't appreciate the distinction. But wait a moment. One of the offences was under Section 9 (1) and the other under Section 12 of the Army Act. 'Ah,' said I, 'I see; he didn't fail to join his Battalion in the line when ordered to do so, but when it was his duty to do so.' 'That's it,' came the triumphant reply, 'you have confused Section 9 (1) with Section 12.' Oh, the official mind! 'May I ask,' I said, 'whether the penalty may be death in each case?' 'Oh yes,' said the great man, 'but Section 9 (1) and Section 12'! Let me say at once that the Director of Personnel Services is a distinguished soldier, and the essence of what is implied in the phrase 'an officer and a gentleman'. But, all the same, as he hugged that sacred manual, with his aristocratic fingers still pointing to Sections 9 (1) and 12, I wondered whether, when in the field (where he has had a brilliant career) he regulated his tactics by the same rule of thumb – or, shall I say, of finger? Again and again I was assured that to the soldier the distinction between the two offences was fundamental – and that was the first of 'the true facts of the case'! I did my best to appear impressed – eager to get to the evidence on which the boy was shot.

A Sacrosanct Record

And what do you think happened? 'No,' said the Director, 'nobody is allowed to see that. In fact, it is because the Record of Proceedings is absolutely private,

and could not be produced even in Court, that the proposed prosecution of you had to be abandoned.' I
confess I was staggered. 'Private,' said I, 'isn't every
Court Martial open to the public? Couldn't I have been
present if the Court Martial had occurred when I was
in France, and taken a full note of the proceedings;
couldn't they have been reported in the Press?' 'Yes, that
is so,' replied the Oracle; 'but Section 124, you know!'
'And what the dickens has Section 124 to do with it?' I
inquired. 'Listen, and you shall hear it,' came the
answer. 'That Section provides that the accused may be
furnished with a copy of the evidence.' 'And he is dead,'
I said, recalling the sapient comment of Mr Macpherson
in the House of Commons a few weeks ago, when he
made that fact an excuse for withholding a copy of the
proceedings from an inquiring Member. 'Quite so,'
again. 'But how on earth does the fact that an accused
person is entitled to a copy of a certain document – relating to a public trial – make it illegal to supply a copy to
anybody else, on payment for such copy; and where do
you get your law that even in a criminal prosecution
such record could not be produced?' And I was assured
that the Law Officers were responsible for that view!
The dossier was solemnly moved out of my reach – and
we have to look elsewhere for 'the true facts of the case'.
I had said that the young officer had no fair chance of
instructing his counsel. But here was a letter from the
Prosecutor, saying that the boy and his counsel were in
conference from 11 to 3 on the day before the Court
Martial. Surely that was conclusive. 'Suppose I have
irrefutable evidence to the effect that he never saw the
boy till the night before the trial, and even then was
unable to get the Summary of Evidence till the following morning?' The director appeared a bit non-plussed
– simply remarking, 'Well of course, we can't say.' You
see, I was waiting for 'the true facts' – and the proposed
counts of the Indictment against me! I was by this time
becoming a little weary of all this verbal quibbling, and
was glad to get to something more substantial.

Recommended to Mercy

In my first article I had laid emphasis on the point that, although found guilty and sentenced to death, there was a strong recommendation to mercy, and I had asked: 'What became of that recommendation?' – adding, 'That needs answering.' Now let me remind you that the members of a Court Martial are both judges and jury, and that as such they had made this strong recommendation to mercy – despite which, in the end, the poor lad was shot. Well, what do you think was the official reply? The recommendation was submitted in turn to officer after officer, in ascending superiority, not one of whom had been a member of the court: yet each of whom was asked to give his opinion as to whether the sentence should be carried out. Some said one thing and some said another – with the result that in the end, the sentence was confirmed by the Commander-in-Chief – and you know the rest. And that was considered a triumphant answer to my question! Five officers, who heard the case and saw the witnesses, unanimous for mercy – and who shied at the responsibility for an unconditional sentence of death – thrust aside by the cold, official 'review' of that Record of Proceedings which cannot be produced, even in a Court of Law! And so I leave all these official explanations – all these threats of prosecution – under DORA. None of them any terror for me. If the authorities think that I have exceeded my functions, let them test public opinion by taking me to the Courts. By the provisions of the Act, I should be deprived of the right of trial by jury – Summary Jurisdiction, with an appeal to a Court of Judges only, being the procedure. But there is the jury of the British public, and the British Army – and of their verdict I have no doubt. And that brings me back to what, after all, is the main point in my case. I claim the right, in all cases of Courts Martial, of an appeal from the death sentence. I would have no exception to that rule. The soldier must not be in a worse position than the civilian. The deterrent effect of the death sentence is secured by its formal promulgation throughout the ranks of the Army; there is no need for haste in carrying it out. What is the reply of the Government to that demand? Here is the callous, cruel answer, given in the House of Commons by Mr Macpherson, to a suggestion by Mr Morrell MP – to whom all honour! – that the King's Regulations affecting trial by Court Martial should be so amended 'as to provide for a right of appeal in special cases': 'The proposal contained in the question could not be effected by Regulation but only by legislation. It is not proposed to introduce legislation for this purpose.' Why not? Would there be any opposition to such legislation? The thing could be done by a one-clause Bill, which could be passed through all its stages, in both Houses, in a day. If it were a matter of curtailing the liberties of the people, or making a grant to a Prince, or an Indemnity to a Minister, it would be done in the twinkling of an eye. But this is only the life of a boy – with a line of patriotic ancestors of whom the proudest in the land might well boast. Poor lad – God rest his soul! And from today let no young fellow holding the King's Commission fear that he is at the mercy of cold, bloodless, unromantic officialism. In no spirit of brag, but with a deep and sincere sense of sacred duty – prompted by an everlasting gratitude for all the boys have done to save us from a foul fate at the hands of a savage foe – I declare that from henceforward, to the end of the tragedy of this war, *John Bull* shall be the Tribune of the soldier, whatever his rank. To Hell with Manuals and Regulations!

Let Them Prosecute!

What does it all come to? My plea for full justice and common humanity stands. I declare it to be scandalous – yes, an infamy – that young and ardent souls, who leaped to the Colours at the call of country, should be subjected to the awful ignominy of the death sentence without a trial in complete conformity with British rules of justice, and without that right which our Civil law now offers to the foulest criminal, of an appeal to a higher Court. And, what is more, I declare it to be a travesty of that humanity which is the basis of British justice that an accused man should be sentenced in his absence, and that he should be wholly ignorant of the awful fate hanging over his head until twelve hours – or less – of that ordeal by fire in the cold grey dawn. Let me say here that if for the moment nothing else is gained by my revelations under that title 'Shot at Dawn', this at least is possible – that the unwittingly callous rule which hides the truth from the accused may be abrogated in favour of a plan by which the sentence is promulgated before the Court Martial closes. It is true that the decision of the Court does not reach finality until it is confirmed by the Commander-in-Chief. But it is surely more merciful that the unhappy man should know the verdict and not be kept in ignorance of his fate until the eve of the dawn which is to fling his soul into the Great Unknown. Never let it be forgotten that we are today dealing not with seasoned soldiers – not with a military caste standing apart from the civilian population, but with a citizen army composed of the best that our cities, our towns and our countryside can offer on the great altar of war, and for the safety and sanctity of our homes. If ever there was a time when the true dictates of humanity and the full founts of justice should be recognized, it is today. I am no advocate for the abolition of capital punishment – it is the ultimate sanction of military discipline. But I warn the Government that the growing public feeling against the infliction of the death penalty can only be satisfied by the assurance that no bloodless red tape, no soulless officaldom, no musty Manuals or rigid Regulations are allowed to prevail in the field. Well, as I have said, I have already said, I have nothing to recant: and if the authorities like to prosecute me, let them do so – for I am convinced that by such means I should the more speedily win my fight for justice and for mercy for the lads at the front – the lads who bleed and die for us all.[7]

The challenge was not taken up, there was no prosecution.

The debate next moved to 14 March, 1918, during the Consolidated Fund Bill debate. Detail of Dyett's case had been outlined this time by William Pringle, Liberal MP for North-West Lanarkshire, resulting in Macpherson replying to the points raised. He said:

> The next complaint of my hon. and learned Friend was that there was no counsel at the preliminary investigation, and he went on to say that very often in civil life, on the criminal side, the preliminary investigation by a stipendiary magistrate results in the charge being dismissed. That is perfectly true. But it is equally true in the case of the soldier.
>
> Let me tell the House in a very few words what actually does happen. The accused is taken before his commanding officer and the evidence against him is given by witnesses, sometimes it is oral evidence and sometimes it is a written statement. The rules of evidence do not apply, however, because the proceedings are non-judicial. If the commanding officer is of opinion that the case is one which does not warrant the accused being discharged or one which he can deal with summarily, he may adjourn the case and have the evidence reduced to writing, with the sole object of forwarding it to a superior authority so that directions of that authority may be received in regard to it.
>
> The superior authority has to form an opinion as to whether or no an offence is disclosed under the Army Act and whether it is possible that the evidence would support such a charge. If the superior authority is satisfied on this point, it is open to him to direct the accused to be tried by court martial or, on the other hand it is open to him to dismiss the case . . .
>
> My hon. Friend complains there was no counsel present at the investigation to begin with. I do not think, in view of what I have said, that it is highly important that counsel should be then present. This way of collecting

the summary of evidence has for a long time been the established practice in the Army, and I understand it is a practice which meets with general favour among both officers and men. My hon. and learned Friend also complained very bitterly that the accused's friend had no copy of the evidence until half an hour before the trial. It is the established practice that the moment a summary of evidence is taken in the way I have described, a copy of it is by order handed to the accused person, and I for one cannot understand why if, as is admitted now, two days before the trial the accused and the accused's friend were in long consultation for four hours on the Sunday, the accused did not produce a copy of that summary of evidence which he was bound in law to have.

Mr Pringle then said: 'Is there any evidence that he did have it?'

The Under-Secretary replied:

I do not know anything about that, but I am almost certain that he had, because I believe it is the law that the accused person must have it, in any case he must have known the evidence against him! I have been for some time in the same profession as my hon. and learned Friend, and I am quite certain that if I were called in to defend a man charged on this very grave charge I should first of all ask him whether he had the summary of evidence which it was my duty to see.

Mr Pringle's rejoinder was: 'Just to clear the matter up, may I say that the statement which has been made to me is this, that the prisoner's friend alleged that the prisoner had not in fact a copy of the summary of evidence, and that he was only able to get it within half an hour of the trial?'
Macpherson replied:

If my argument is right that cannot be a reason for blaming the War Office. If the accused, having got the summary of evidence, could not in fact produce it to his counsel two days before the trial the War Office and the Commander-in-Chief in France ought not to be blamed. I am told, on what I regard as most reliable authority, that in every case, particularly in the case of sentence of death, the summary of evidence is always handed to the accused person.[8]

So there we have it. The Under-Secretary of State for War who, on 20 February had asked for time so he could have all the facts of the case fully investigated, on 6 March said that he had made such enquiries; and on the 14th having had the benefit of seeing the court-martial file said, regarding the Summary of Evidence, 'I am almost certain that he had, because it is the law that the accused person must have it'. And further he said the immortal words, 'In any case he must have known the evidence against him'.

References

1. Putkowski, Julian and Sykes, Julian, *Shot at Dawn*, Leo Cooper, 1989, p. 155.
2. *John Bull*, 23 February, 1918.
3. House of Lords, Record Office: HC Deb. 5th Series, Vol. 103, 20 February, 1918, cc 846–50.
4. House of Lords, Record Office: HC Deb, 5th Series, Vol. 103, 20 February, 1918, c 850.
5. *John Bull*, 2 March, 1918.
6. House of Lords, Record Office: HC Deb, 5th Series, Vol. 103, 6 March, 1918, cc 1954–5.
7. *John Bull*, 16 March, 1918.
8. House of Lords, Record Office: HC Deb, 5th Series, Vol. 104, 14 March, 1918, cc 562–72.

CHAPTER EIGHT

The Wind of Change

Before England had a standing army, in times of peace there was no necessity for a military code. On the outbreak of war, 'ordinances' or 'articles of war' were issued by the Crown or the Army Commander under royal authority. Once hostilities ended, the army was disbanded and with it the articles also ended.

The first record of an 'ordinance' referring to the Military is thought to be by Richard I at the start of the Crusades:

> Made at Chinon, 1st Richard, 1169. Charter of King Richard for the Government of those going by sea to the Holy Land.
>
> Richard by the grace of God, King of England, Duke of Burgundy, etc. – To all his men going by sea to Jerusalem, greeting. Know ye, by the common council of all good men, we have made the underwritten ordinances.
>
> He who kills a man on shipboard shall be bound to the dead man and thrown into the sea; if the man is killed on shore, the slayer shall be bound to the dead body and buried with it. Anyone convicted by lawful witnesses of having drawn his knife to strike another, or who shall have drawn blood of him, to lose his hand. If he shall have only struck with the palm of his hand without drawing blood, he shall be thrice ducked in the sea. Any man who shall reproach, abuse or curse his companion shall, for every time he is convicted thereof, give him so many ounces of silver. Anyone convicted of theft

shall be shorn like a champion, boiling pitch shall be poured on his head and down of feathers shaken over it, that he may be known, and he shall be set ashore at the first land at which the ship touches.[1]

Other articles on record are those during the reign of Richard II and Henry V during the war with France. When in 1660 a standing army was established and, due to the rapid growth in its numbers and power, there developed much scepticism and disquiet within Parliament. It was found necessary to have articles and regulations to govern it, but, due to Parliament's distrust, these were never sanctioned, and the special powers authorized by the Crown proved deficient in maintaining good discipline.

Punishments were harsh. Death, maiming, the fracturing of limbs, boring of the tongue with a red-hot iron were all part of the military code of 1642. Burning or branding the cheek and cutting off the left ear were also used to instil discipline. On occasions lots were drawn to choose which offender would be executed.

Later discipline declined and became very lax, resulting in 1689 in the First Mutiny Act 'For the Better Regulation of the Discipline in the Army'. This was the first statutory military law in times of peace. This legislation upheld the punishment of the loss of life or limb within the shores of the United Kingdom. The passage of the bill was hurried through when two Scots regiments mutinied at Ipswich, when they were ordered to depart for Holland and refused to go and began to march north, stating that James II was their rightful King. They were brought to heel by three regiments of Dutch dragoons.

This bill made the offence of mutiny and desertion punishable by the death penalty and set up courts martial. The intention was for it to be limited to just seven months; however, it was renewed annually, except for a few intervals, until 1878. The original legislation applied only to England and Wales, but was extended by stages to cover Ireland in 1702, Scotland in 1707, the Colonies in 1718 and the rest of the world in 1803.

In 1712 statutory power was given to the Crown to make Articles of War under the Royal prerogative. These were gradually encroached upon, as it proved somewhat of an inconvenience to have the army subject partly to a statutory act and partly to articles. In 1803 the Mutiny Act and Statutory Articles were extended to the military within or without the dominions of the Crown. From that time on the Crown lost its prerogative, as the army was now to be governed only by statutory law.

By 1879 Articles of War and the powers of the Mutiny Act were consolidated in the Army Discipline Act of 1879, which was repealed and, with amendments, re-enacted in the Army Act of 1881. This is brought into operation each year by passing the Annual Army Act.

In the First World War death was the maximum punishment for the following offences:

Section	Headings	Crime	
4	offences in relation to the enemy	1	shamefully abandoning post
		2	shamefully casting away arms
		3	treacherously holding correspondence with the enemy
		4	assisting or harbouring enemy
		5	voluntarily aiding enemy when a prisoner of war
		6	knowingly committing an act which imperils the success of the forces
		7	cowardly misbehaviour before enemy
6	offences committed on active service which are punishable more severely on active service than at other times. (otherwise by cashiering or imprisonment)	1	leaving commanding officer to plunder
		2	leaving guard or post without orders
		3	forcing safeguard
		4	forcing or striking sentinel
		5	impeding or refusing to assist provost-marshal
		6	using violence to bringer of supplies or person, or property of inhabitants
		7	breaking into a place to plunder
		8	intentionally causing false alarms
		9	treachery about parole, watchword, or countersign

		10 irregularly appropriating supplies contrary to orders
		11 sleeps on, is drunk on, or leaves his post when a sentry
7	special offences	(a) mutiny and sedition
12		(b) desertion (on active service)
8		(c) violence to a superior officer in execution of his office
9		(d) wilful defiance in disobeying the lawful command given personally by superior officer in execution of his office

The military handbook, *Military Law: Its Procedure and Practice*, produced for officers and non-commissioned officers, outlines the history of courts martial in the 1910 edition, as follows:

> The administration of the military code in the first instance under Articles of War, and subsequently under both the Mutiny Act and Articles of War, was carried out by means of military courts. The first of these appears to have been the *Curia Militaris*, or Court of Chivalry, which was part of the Aula Regia, or supreme court of great officers of State, established by William the Conqueror.
>
> The Court of Chivalry consisted of the Lord High Constable, who was the King's general and Commander-in-Chief, and the Earl Marshal, whose duty it was to marshal the army, and ascertain that all persons liable to serve fulfilled their liabilities.
>
> > To the constable it appertaineth to have cognizance of all contracts and deeds of arms, and of our war out of the realm, and also of things that touch war within the realm, which cannot be determined by common law.
> >
> > All appeals of things done within the realm shall be tried and determined by the good laws of the realm made and used in the time of the King's

noble progenitors, and all appeals to be made of things done out of the realm shall be tried and determined before the constable and marshal of England for the time being.

In the time of war the court of the constable, as it was usually called, followed the army, and punished summarily accordingly to the Articles of War for the time being in force.

It is evident that a single court was incapable of dealing with troops acting in different places, and additional constables and marshals were delegated by commission from the Crown to form other courts when required.

The office of High Constable was abolished in the reign of Henry VIII, and with it lapsed all the criminal jurisdiction of the Court of Chivalry. With the concurrence of the judges of the common law, the marshal occasionally held a court himself on purely civil matters, but the jurisdiction and power of punishment of the court were so limited that, although never legally abolished, it became extinct.

From the abolition of the office of the hereditary High Constable up to the recognition of the military courts by statute in 1689, military law was administered by means of commissioners, by the general in command of the troops himself sitting as marshal or by means of deputies whom he was authorized to appoint.

The commissioners or deputies were usually officers of the army and, at the beginning of the great civil rebellion, habitually formed courts or councils of war, in accordance with the then existing continental military jurisprudence.

These councils of war some few years prior to the passing of the Mutiny Act were called courts martial and, with slight modifications as to constitution and power, are the existing military courts. In the earlier courts martial the general or governor of the garrison who convened the court ordinarily sat as president, the power of the court was plenary, and the sentences were

carried into execution without the confirmation
required under the present law[2]

The Darling Committee

In 1919 the Darling Committee was set up to enquire into
the law and rules of procedure regulating military courts
martial. Named after its Chairman, The Right Hon. Sir
Charles Darling, it had a membership of twelve, including
the champion of Edwin Dyett, Horatio Bottomley MP. It
sat for some twenty-two days, hearing evidence from a
number of witnesses and receiving written submissions.

A very illuminating comment on it can be found on a
minute sheet of the Air Ministry:

> The report of the Military Courts Martial Committee
> has been held four years too late. During the war, with
> its expansion and consequent irregularities perpetrated
> by regimental and staff officers with only an elementary
> knowledge of Air Force Law, a great many faults in the
> Courts Martial system have assumed proportions which
> are not justified with normal conditions.

The committee found that, after the first few months of the
war, the loss of so many regular officers who were familiar
with military law and the urgent need for reinforcements
made it almost impossible to devote much attention to the
legal training of new recruits. Additionally, the fact that a
large number of trials were conducted in close proximity to
the enemy in circumstances calculated to enhance the difficulties and that officers could be ill spared from their other
urgent duties could have an adverse effect.

The Committee's enquiries were wide-ranging and covered such aspects as the legal knowledge of officers, arrest,
civil offences, summary of evidence, provision of copy of
charge, publicity of trials, courts and their composition,
independence of courts martial, prosecution evidence,
recording proceedings, form of record, decision of the
court, announcement of finding and sentence, confirm-

ation, promulgation, punishments, the Suspension of Sentences Act, right to a copy of proceedings and a number of other matters, some of which I highlight below:

Delay

On this point the committee stated:

> In France, for example, an offensive might last for days, or even weeks, and until its conclusion it was impossible to bring witnesses out of the line. When it was concluded it was more than likely that some of the witnesses would be found to be casualties, and a further delay would be thereby rendered inevitable.
>
> After making all allowance for the circumstances there has undoubtedly been undue delay in some cases – mostly in cases of officers.

Preparation of defence

Para 47 stated:

> We also recommend that in every case the accused be specifically asked immediately after arraignment whether he has had time to prepare his defence, and whether (and if so, why) he wishes for an adjournment, and that his answers be recorded.

Counsel

When inquiring into the role of counsel it stated:

> At present an accused person may have his defence conducted by a barrister or solicitor, or by an officer. We have received a suggestion that any person subject to military law should be allowed to act as counsel. With this we do not agree. If the person were a barrister or solicitor or competent officer, he could so act at present. If he were not, it is not likely that he would be of real

assistance to the accused or to the court. Amateur lawyers have defects of their own; and we entirely agree with the opinion that a poor advocate is worse than useless, and frequently injures his client's case. This fact is well recognized by those concerned in the work of ordinary civil courts.

We agree, however, with the suggestion put forward by the Judge Advocate General for assigning competent counsel to an accused who is remanded for trial, and who does not wish to defend himself or to rely upon someone selected by himself.

The right to have an advocate thus assigned should be embodied in a Rule of Procedure, which should make it clear that such right does not derogate from the right of the accused to be assisted or represented by a friend or counsel selected by himself, and does not relieve the Court in any way of its responsibility for safeguarding his interests. *This right should be absolute unless, on active service, or outside the United Kingdom or India,* the Convening Officer certifies that no suitable officer is available.

Evidence has been given before us to the effect that in some instances superior authorities have actively discouraged officers from appearing on behalf of accused persons. In our opinion serious notice should be taken of any such practice. An officer should feel himself at perfect liberty to defend any man of his unit or company if asked to do so. At the same time we regard it as undesirable, and contrary to the best interests of discipline, that any officer at a station should seek or acquire the reputation of being the 'prisoner's friend', anxious to appear in Court on behalf of all and sundry.

Appeal

The committee considered the desirability of giving a right of appeal 1. in all cases of trial by court martial, or 2. in the case of death sentences. It compared the respective rights of a soldier convicted by court martial and of a man convicted upon indictment in a civil court. It stated: 'that in the case of a man convicted upon indictment, unless he himself takes some action, there is no review of the proceedings. Whatever informality, error of fact or illegality may have occurred, only the formal record of conviction remains.'

When a judge passes a capital sentence he informs the Home Secretary of the fact, and the case is considered in the Home Office as a matter of course. In other cases there is a review by the Home Office, if a petition is presented, or by the Court of Criminal Appeal if an appeal is lodged, or a certificate raising a point of law is granted by the Judge at the trial.

A soldier is in a better position. The proceedings are first considered before confirmation by the confirming authority, who has to satisfy himself as to the finding and that the sentence is not excessive; if he is not satisfied on both points, he either declines to confirm, or reduces the sentence (as the case may be). Further, in the case of a conviction, he can send back the finding and sentence for revision, but the sentence cannot be increased.

After confirmation the Proceedings are forwarded to the Judge Advocate General's Office where, unless that Office has previously advised as to the propriety of confirmation, they are again reviewed independently, and the legality of the conviction considered.

In addition, if a soldier is not satisfied with this automatic review, he can present a petition, upon receipt of which the proceedings are again reconsidered. It is possible, however, that all soldiers are not aware that any petition against the legality of a conviction or the severity of a sentence will be considered. We think that a definite statement to this effect should be included in the King's Regulations; and, in the case of death sentence, we think such a statement should be added to Army Form W. 3996.

We are of opinion that it is undesirable to set up any formal Court of Appeal from the decisions of courts martial, since these courts sit and adjudicate in circumstances wholly different from those in which the civil courts exercise their power. So far as findings are concerned, the court who actually see and hear the witnesses are far more likely to arrive at a correct conclusion upon conflicting evidence than any Appellate Tribunal. The best method of minimizing the risk of error is, in our opinion, not to set up a Court of Appeal, but to strengthen as far as possible the trial court.

In regard to sentences, we consider that, subject to the right to petition for clemency, the decision ought to be left, as at present, to the military authorities, who alone are in a position to form a correct judgment as to what sentences the state of discipline in the army, or a particular force requires. Nor do we consider that any exception ought to be made in the case of death sentences. During the recent war not a single officer or soldier was executed under sentence of court martial in the United Kingdom. Abroad a certain number of death sentences were carried out. In each case they were only carried out after personal consideration by, and upon orders of, the Commander-in-Chief, and after the Judge Advocate General, or his Deputy, had advised upon their legality. Moreover, when considering them, the Commander-in-Chief almost invariably had before him recommendations from the officers commanding the unit to which the accused belonged, the Brigade, the Division, the Corps and the Army.

As showing the care with which all considerations were weighed and the desire to show mercy whenever the interests of the Army as a whole, and of the nation, permitted, it may be stated that no fewer than 89 per cent of death sentences pronounced were commuted by the Commander-in-Chief. We doubt very much whether any Court, necessarily not possessing the information which he possessed as to the discipline and morale of the army, would have ventured to exercise clemency to any such extent. The Commander-in-Chief, of course, commuted sentences in many cases where the Court of

Criminal Appeal would have had no legal grounds for interfering, and must therefore have dismissed an appeal.

The reasons for punishing crime on conviction in the Civil Courts are the amendment of offenders, the deterrent effect of punishment and the satisfaction of the outraged sentiment of the people, who otherwise would be apt to take private vengeance after slight injury and no proof. For the punishing of military offences there is the further reason that, unless discipline in Armies be preserved, such forces are but a mob dangerous to all but the enemies of their country. Therefore the considerations sufficient for civil government are not enough for the ruling of the armed forces of the Crown. On active service, especially, other sanctions must be sought when justice is to be done.

The principles upon which punishments for military offences are inflicted remain the same now as when the Duke of Wellington in 1814 wrote as follows:

> I consider all punishments to be for the sake of example, and the punishment of military men in particular is expedient only in cases where the prevalence of any crime, or the evils resulting from it, are likely to be injurious to the public interests.
>
> I beg the Court to consider their recommendations in this light and to apply it to the existing circumstances and situation of the Army, and to what is notorious in regard to this crime . . .
>
> I beg to inform the court martial that a very common, and a most alarming, crime in this Army is that of striking and otherwise resisting, sometimes even by firing at, non-commissioned officers, and even officers, in the execution of their duty. It will not be disputed that there is no crime so fatal to the very existence of an Army, and no crime which officers, sworn as the members of a general court martial are, should feel so

anxious to punish, as that of which this soldier has been guilty.

It is very unpleasant to me to be obliged to resist the inclination of the general court martial to save the life of this soldier; but I would wish the Court to observe that, if the impunity with which this offence, clearly proved, shall have been committed, should, as is possible, occasion resistance to authority in other instances, the supposed mercy will turn out to be extreme cruelty, and will occasion the loss of some valuable men to the service.

The committee completed their report with the following comments:

In our opinion a Commander-in-Chief, who is entrusted with the safety of his Army, must not be fettered in his decision as to the point which so vitally affects the discipline of that Army. The essence of military punishments is that they should be exemplary and speedy. This is recognized by the preamble to the Mutiny Acts and the Army Acts which have been passed annually by Parliament for centuries. An exemplary punishment speedily carried out may prevent a mutiny from spreading or save an Army from defeat.

However, a minority report was signed by three members of the committee, one of whom was Horatio Bottomley MP. They made a number of points and were of the opinion that: 'In the field there should be no Court of Appeal, except in the cases of death sentences.' Their report opened with the following remarks:

Under the ruling of the Chairman, the Committee decided that the Terms of Reference precluded them from investigating the facts and merits of any particular court martial trials, except in so far as they threw light upon the present law and procedure of courts martial.

Consequently, it has not fully investigated cases of alleged miscarriage of justice. It has, however, taken evidence of hardship and irregularities arising out of the existing practice. It was, in our opinion, abundantly proved that cases occurred of irregularity in the taking of Summaries of Evidence, in the proceedings of courts martial themselves, and even during the stages which intervene before the proceedings are eventually reviewed by the Judge Advocate General.[3]

The evidence that was brought before the Darling Committee was never made public, so what the irregularities or suggested miscarriages of justice were we will never know.

Enquiry into 'Shell-shock'

In the light of the growing unease in both the public and in Parliament, on 28 April, 1920, Lord Southborough requested that the government set up an enquiry into a condition known commonly as 'shell-shock'. As a result, on 12 August of that year, the Army Council submitted its terms of reference for such an enquiry. It was to be under the Chairmanship of Lord Southborough himself and was to consist of fourteen members from such interested departments as the Admiralty, Air Ministry, Board of Control, Ministry of Pensions, Board of Control for Scotland, War Office, Army and Members of Parliament. It sat for the first time on 7 September, 1920; during the course of forty-one sittings it examined fifty-nine witnesses.

The evidence given was from distinguished representatives of the military, service medical authorities, and the general medical profession. The legal aspects of the case were not forgotten. However, the inquiry lacked in its own words, 'Any reliable statistics covering cases of "shell-shock". Much statistical matter was unavoidably lost during the progress of the war, and other material of a statistical kind, buried in the archives of the War Office and other Departments is at present inaccessible and the

Committee were advised by Lieutenant-General Sir John Goodwin that it could not, in fact, be obtained without a prohibitive amount of labour and expense and an expiration of time which would have postponed our report.'

The report was, therefore, somewhat limited from the start. It concluded that shell-shock was not a new condition, stating:

> For this purpose we had to decide what 'shell-shock' is and what it is not. Without going too deeply into the history of the origin of the term, we conclude that it was born of the necessity for finding at the moment some designation thought to be suitable for the number of cases of functional nervous incapacity which were continually occurring among the fighting units. Undoubtedly 'shell-shock' signified in the popular mind that the patient had been exposed to, and had suffered from, the physical effects of explosion of projectiles. Had this explanation of the various conditions held good, no fundamental fault could have been found with the term. But with the extension of voluntary enlistment, and afterwards the introduction of conscription, it was discovered that nervous disorders, neurosis and hysteria, which had appeared to a small degree in the Regular Army, were becoming astoundingly numerous from causes other than shock caused by the bursting of high explosives. It was observed in fact that these conditions were perpetually occurring although the patient had not suffered from commotional disturbance of the nervous system caused by bursting shells. It even became apparent that numerous cases of 'shell-shock' were coming under the notice of the medical authorities where the evidence indicated that the patients had not even been within hearing of a shell-burst. On the other hand, it became abundantly plain to the medical profession that in very many cases the change from civil life brought about by enlistment and physical training was sufficient to cause neurasthenic and hysterical symptoms, and that the wear and tear of a prolonged

campaign of trench warfare with its terrible hardships and anxieties, and of attack and perhaps repulse, produced a condition of mind and body properly falling under the term 'war neurosis', practically indistinguishable from the forms of neurosis known to every doctor under ordinary conditions of civil life.

The Committee recognized, therefore, from the outset of the inquiry that the term 'shell-shock' was wholly misleading, but unfortunately its use had been established and the harm was already done. The alliteration and dramatic significance of the term had caught the public imagination, and thenceforward there was no escape from its use.[4]

General Sir Philip Christison who was a machine-gun officer in the First World War highlights this point, as follows:

I remember a corporal, in my Company, who was the Battalion heavyweight boxing champion, and a very powerfully built fellow. He came to me before one battle and he said, 'I can't face it!'

So I said, 'Come on, you can't let your men down, you are a corporal, you have got to lead your section.'

He said, 'I have had enough, I can't face it. If you want to court-martial me, you can.'

And so I referred this to the CO. He was removed and he was court-martialled and was sentenced to death, but the sentence was suspended. But I always remember that, because one of my very clear ideas was this question of man management, in war and battle. It was going to stand me in tremendous stead in World War Two, when we did have psychologists on our staff and knew how to deal with stress before it got too late. In the First World War we didn't, and were apt to class stress relapse as cowardice, when in effect it was a nervous condition, which might happen to anybody, and indeed which happened to myself, in World War One. Ever since then I realized how important it was to judge how much men, or an officer, or a general could take, without losing efficiency and appearing to be a coward.[5]

References

1. Thurtle, Ernest, *Military Discipline and Democracy*, C.W. Daniel, 1920, p. 1.
2. Sisson, Lieut.-Col. C. Pratt, RA, *Military Law*, Kegan Paul, Trench, Trubner, 1910, pp. 3–7, 138–9.
3. Public Record Office, Kew, ref. AIR 2/104/A15452: Darling Committee Military Committee, 1919.
4. House of Lords, Record Office: Report on War Office Committee of Enquiry into 'Shell-Shock' 1922, HC Sessional Papers, Accounts and Papers 2. XII 1922, p. 788.
5. Liddle Collection, Leeds University: Tape 334b, December, 1975.

CHAPTER NINE

Much Soul-Searching

In 1925 a report of the Interdepartmental Committee on Proposed Disciplinary Amendments of the Army and Air Force Acts, under the Chairmanship of J.J. Lawson, was published. It stated:

> The main grounds on which the abolition of the death penalty on active service is urged may, we think, be summarized as follows:

> That there have been miscarriages of justice owing to failure to distinguish between real cowardice and physical breakdown, or owing to harsh or unfair conduct of trials;

> That other penalties, combined with moral pressure, would be equally or more efficacious;

> And that the code of military law is in itself unduly severe, and is unequal as between officers and other ranks.

It found:

> We do not think that any actual case of miscarriage of justice was substantiated before us. The alleged instances brought to notice were not large . . . [it found] particulars given in comparison with records to be frequently inaccurate or incomplete.

It is hardly surprising that witnesses' evidence was somewhat inaccurate and incomplete. They did not have the benefit of the court-martial files. But how could such a committee state: 'We do not *think* [my italics] that any actual case of miscarriage of justice was substantiated before us.'? A little word, but it speaks volumes.

The report continued:

> As to alleged differentiation in favour of officers, it may be pointed out that all ranks, including officers, are at all times equally required to obey all lawful commands; that in war all ranks, including officers, are equally deprived of the option of leaving the service; and lastly that all ranks, including officers, are equally liable to incur the death penalty for each of the offences for which it is authorized.[1]

In theory this is correct, but in practical terms it glosses over the subject, as only three officers were executed in the Great War, one for the offence of murder.

The Committee was in agreement with the Darling Committee that there should be no right of appeal to a civil court, and that the death sentence be retained for the more serious offences only. In the 1928 Army and Air Force Act changes were made abolishing the death penalty for a number of less serious offences still left on the statute book, as follows:

1 leaving his commanding officer to go in search of plunder
2 forcing a safeguard
3 forcing or striking a sentinel
4 breaking into any house or other place in search of plunder
5 being a soldier acting as sentinel sleeps or is drunk on his post
6 striking or offering violence to a superior officer
7 disobeying an order in such a manner as to show defiance

8 altering or interfering with air signals without
   authority

Thus capital crimes were reduced to desertion, cowardice,
mutiny, treachery and leaving a guard or post without
orders.

In June, 1929, there was a general election, which left no
party with an absolute majority. The House now consisted
of 288 Labour MPs, 260 Conservatives and 59 Liberals.
Ramsay MacDonald, with Liberal support, formed his
second Labour Government. In April, 1930, the Army and
Air Force Act came up for its annual review. Change was
again in the air, after extensive lobbying by the MP Ernest
Thurtle and others. Tom Shaw, the Secretary of State for
War, went against the advice of the Army Council and proposed that the offences of cowardice and leaving a post
without orders should cease to be capital offences.
However, he confirmed that desertion would remain an
offence punishable by death.
   Thurtle was not to be put off, and moved an amendment to
substitute penal servitude for the death penalty for desertion.
If carried, this would have a most dramatic effect in reducing
executions as, during the Great War, of the 346 men executed,
266 were for this offence. The passing of this amendment
would have almost abolished the ultimate penalty.
   The argument ebbed and flowed, and the government
allowed a free vote on the amendment. It was passed by 219
votes to 135. This meant that the only offences subject to
death were mutiny and treachery. It is interesting to note
that, during the various votes taken on the matter, members
with a service background (i.e. those with military or naval
titles in the tellers' listings) came down very strongly in
favour of maintaining the status quo.

	In favour of retention	Military titles
Total vote 453	165	57
	In favour of abolition	Military titles
	288	11

	In favour of retention	Military titles
Total vote 354	135	55
	In favour of abolition	Military titles
	219	7

	In favour of retention	Military titles
Total vote 244	50	22
	In favour of abolition	Military titles
	194	4

The debate showed very strong feelings on both sides of the argument. In order to highlight some of the opinions held, here are a number of extracts from the large number of speeches made during this highly emotional debate:

Sir Lambert Ward stated:

> Many years ago a famous American soldier described war. He was General Ulysses Grant who commanded the Federal Forces during the later days of the American Civil War. He was a man of very few words, and he said: 'War is just hell'. What we are discussing tonight is just one small corner of what, in my opinion, can never be anything else but hell, especially to the ordinary private soldier in an infantry battalion. As one rises in the ranks, although responsibility increases, war becomes much less hellish . . . .
>
> There is one simple axiom with regard to this problem and it is this. There is no justice in the death penalty any more than there is justice in war. War is the absolute negation of justice and equity; and, if a Government is foolish enough to go to war, the nation has to win that war, or else the state of a country such as this would be too terrible to contemplate.

Lieutenant-Colonel Sir Arthur Pelham Heneage followed:

> I share with my hon. and gallant Friend the hope that we shall not have any more wars, and certainly not in

this generation; but, if there are any more wars, we are setting a dangerous precedent entirely to eliminate cowardice from the death penalty. If we eliminate cowardice, there is no penalty so drastic to be imposed as the penalty to which a man who is not a coward is liable by remaining under fire.

The elimination of cowardice from the death penalty has been tried before, and it showed that there was a distinct danger of the rank and file taking matters into their own hands.

Major-General Sir Robert Hutchison said:

As an old soldier, I have come to the view which the Secretary of State for War has taken, and therefore I welcome the alteration in the Army Act in respect of the offence of cowardice. After all, anyone who has had service in the field knows the extraordinary strain under which men, and especially private soldiers, suffer, and I look upon a man whose brain goes under that stress as being wounded – wounded mentally.

Major John Mills continued:

I know that you cannot look into a man's heart and see what influences are at work, but I should be surprised if any man said to himself, 'I shall go forward, because the man on my right and the man on my left will go forward as well or else they will be shot . . . .'

Where a man is engaged regularly in the army you might be right in shooting him for cowardice, but you have not the same right in the case of civilian volunteers. You have no right to take a man from the factory or the farm and put him into khaki and a tin hat, and then shoot him if he shows cowardice.

Mr Geoffrey Shaw stated:

There may have been a romance in war when man met

man, and when a man could see his enemy and fight his enemy. There is no romance in mud, vermin, and shell and shot, where men are destroyed without a possible chance of seeing the enemy they are fighting. There is no romance in that; it is simply brutality, dirt, disease and death.

Mr Robert Morrison said:

Time after time we return to the point that expert opinion is against it, but I would remind the right hon. Gentleman and the Committee that, as far as those of us on these benches who have no inside knowledge of the wonderful and mysterious ways in which expert opinion expresses itself are able to judge, expert opinion was against the abolition of flogging in the army.

Year after year in this House expert opinion stoutly defended what soldiers called crucifixion – Field Punishment No 1 – and year after year representatives of the Government rose from the Front Bench and said that they were advised by expert opinion that Field Punishment No 1 was a deterrent and that it should not be abolished, otherwise discipline would go to pieces. When Field Punishment No 1, flogging in the army, and offence after offence for which the death penalty has been inflicted were abolished, we had exactly the same argument that the discipline of the army would go to pieces.

Rear-Admiral Tufton Beamish followed:

After all, the necessity for success in war is absolutely paramount. One coward may lose a battle, one battle may lose a war, and one war may lose a country. That being so, every possible check should be placed on anything that is going to bring about the loss of a battle or a war. Fear is perfectly natural. It comes to all people. The man who conquers fear is a hero, but the man who is conquered by fear is a coward, and he deserves all he gets.

Ernest Thurtle said:

> There were two Army Corps of Australians fighting in
> the last war, and not a single one of these Australians
> was executed. We executed Englishmen, Welshmen,
> Scotsmen, Canadians, even New Zealanders, but not a
> single Australian was executed. According to the argu-
> ment of the Army Council, in order that discipline
> should be effectively maintained it is necessary to have
> this sanction of the death penalty. What happened in the
> case of the Australians? Does anyone suggest that the
> Australians, although they had not the death penalty
> hanging over their heads to keep them fighting, did not
> behave with just as much gallantry, just as much
> courage, as any of the other troops? If that is so, if it was
> unnecessary to apply this penalty in the case of the
> Australian troops why should it be necessary to apply it
> in the case of the other British troops?
> I say that, if it is demonstrated that the Australian
> troops could fight gallantly and courageously, as they
> did, without the death penalty, then it is a libel on the
> courage of other British troops to say that they will not
> fight without the death penalty.[2]

The Bill now went forward to the House of Lords to be
considered in Committee.

Viscount FitzAlan of Derwent opened:

> I should like to point out that the Secretary of State, in
> the course of his speech in another place, stated very
> frankly and, if I may so with all respect, very properly,
> that in taking the action that he took he was acting con-
> trary to the opinion and the advice of his Army Council.
> They had tried to instil into him that the death penalty
> for cowardice acted as a great deterrent, and that in their
> opinion the mere fact of the death penalty being applic-
> able would not only save men from becoming cowards,
> but would also save other men from losing their lives
> owing to the action which they might take. If they had

only imprisonment in front of them instead of the death penalty, the temptation to perform an act of cowardice would in many cases be almost irresistible.

Viscount Plumer, Commander of Second Army from 1915 to 1918, said:

> I can tell your Lordships from personal experience that there is no more painful duty a commander has to carry out, none which he would more gladly avoid, than signing the death warrant for the execution of one of his own men . . .
>
> If the Bill stands as it is now, I am quite confident that in the future, far distant as that future may be, the effect will be to prejudice the morale and also the high standard of discipline which hitherto has been a proud tradition of the British Army.

Viscount Allenby, Commander of the Army which had defeated the Turks in 1918, said:

> When [the recruit] joins he is well aware of the fact that certain offences in war are liable to the penalty of death. That does not trouble him at all; it causes no alarm to him, because he is young and he does not contemplate the possibility of his committing any of those crimes which would render him liable to that punishment. But the severity of the penalty indicates the enormity of the offence, and it creates a moral atmosphere which causes him to abhor that crime and anything that would affect his honour and duty as a soldier. The moral influence thus created would, I think, be very much lessened if the penalty of death were abolished.

Viscount Mersey, a judge and former MP, then spoke:

> I was Provost Marshal of the army at the Dardanelles and I had a good deal to do with Courts Martial. There is no more human or humane tribunal in the world.

Who are the accused? They are the soldiers of the officers sitting on the Court Martial. They are almost their children. They are the men alongside whom the officers have been fighting and alongside whom they are hoping to fight for the rest of the campaign. Behind them is the confirming authority and in what used to be called a Drumhead Court Martial – a Field General Court Martial . . . .

I will only give two examples. I remember a case in China many years ago. We were fighting alongside several Allies – the incident does not relate to British soldiers. I remember in an entrenched camp which had been taken at night a piquet being put forward with a couple of sentries. The sentries went to sleep. They were killed, and the whole piquet was massacred. That is the sort of thing that may happen. I remember a case in the Dardanelles when a line, after a very hard and miserable two days and nights, began to break, leaving the troops on either side in the air. There were two Second Lieutenants just come out from school. They were the only remaining officers. They took the law into their own hands, because it was the only thing they could do.

The Secretary of State for Air, Lord Thomson, said:

My attitude with regard to the first three offences – cowardice and those allied to it – was based upon what I conceive to be the very great difference between a modern army, and especially a modern volunteer army such as our own, and those armies for which this dreadful code of punishments was drawn up, a code of punishments which has been mitigated through the centuries. It was drawn up either for mercenary troops or for men who so nearly bordered on the criminal classes that the most stringent measures had to be employed to maintain even a semblance of order. But I submit that the difference between the class of man who sacked Badajoz and the young men in our Army today is so great that you cannot apply the same code of laws to those two types.

131

I would say, I think without exaggeration, that the ordinary private soldier in the Army today is ten times as sensitive a human being as those soldiers were. I think I may claim that there are many aircraftmen in the Air Force who are better educated today than the majority of officers were at the time of Waterloo, and I think that many of them are just as well educated as young officers were when I was a young officer. In fact I am certain that I could not pass the examinations that are being passed by aircraftmen today, nor could I have done so at any time of my life. We are dealing with a totally different set of human beings. I submit that it would be impossible, unwise and I am inclined to think impracticable, especially if you enrol these men as a nation in arms, as conscripts in your citizen Army, to expose them to a code of laws totally different from that to which they are accustomed in private life and punish them for offences that are not really crimes of violence, just as you would punish them for murder in a civilian State.

I think it was the noble and gallant Viscount, Lord Plumer, who said that penal servitude means safety to the coward. I think he must have overlooked to some extent the Act that was passed during the war, the Army (Suspension of Sentences) Act. Men did not get back to safety because they had been sentenced to penal servitude for any of the crimes mentioned by Lord FitzAlan. On the contrary, some of the men who had been sentenced to death had their sentences commuted to penal servitude and were sent up to the front again. Cases occurred of men going back two and three times. They did not get back to safety because they were cowards and abandoned their comrades.

When the vote was taken, the Lords by 45 votes to 12 decided to restore the death penalty for desertion, cowardice and leaving a post.[3] The following day the Commons were to consider this turn of events. Captain Robert Bourne, a Conservative backbencher, suggested a compromise that, in view of the Lords' objections, the government should now go forward with only their original intention of abolishing the death penalty for leaving one's post and for cowardice, and overrule the vote in respect of desertion. This would mean that, as this was by far the most frequent offence, capital punishment could still be widely used. Winston Churchill supported this suggestion. However, Ernest Thurtle was not to be thwarted and said:

> I suggest that the House would be sadly lacking in a sense of its own dignity if it were to discuss the merits of this question again. This House is the duly elected representative House of the people and, after considering this question on its merits recently, it came to a unanimous decision on a free vote in favour of the abolition of the death penalty for desertion. In the circumstances, it seems to me arrogance and impertinence and a piece of astounding audacity on the part of another place, which has been described by the right hon. Gentleman the Member for Epping [Mr Churchill] as a worn-out anachronism, to presume to attempt to override the decision of the elected representatives of the people, come to without any hesitation. The House should not demean itself by once again debating the merits of the question and should reject the Lords' Amendment.

The House divided and Thurtle's views won the argument by 194 votes to 50, with the Motion made 'That this House doth disagree with the Lords in the said amendment'. A committee was appointed to draw up reasons to be assigned to the Lords for disagreeing to their Amendments to the Bill, but it transpired that the Lords were not intent in taking the matter any further. The spectre of the firing squad no longer hung over the head of the Briton at arms, unless he should lean towards treachery or mutiny.[4]

The Oliver Committee

We have seen that, after much soul-searching and reflection, legislation was passed which resulted in mutiny and treachery remaining the only offences punishable with death. Still there was much disquiet and annoyance in respect of the system of court martial. As a result, on 18 March, 1938, the Army and Air Force Courts-Martial Committee was set up by the Secretaries of State for War and Air, to examine the existing system of trial by courts martial. The Chairman was Mr (later Sir) Roland Oliver MC, KC. The committee was particularly asked to consider the desirability of appeal by Army and Air Force personnel to a civil tribunal. During its deliberations some 696 letters were to be laid before the committee.[5] Many views were expressed as to whether execution during the First World War and the mode of trial was fair and justified. Here follows a selection of quotations from hard-liners who believed that execution was the only answer to the problem of serious indiscipline:

> ### Letter 214
> When on active service it is of great importance that those accused of offences against the conduct of the war and [of] endangering the safety of their comrades are specially brought to trial and, if convicted, [are] specially punished. This quick disposal of the guilty acts as a deterrent to others who for various reasons may commit similar offences which, if [they became] widespread [would] lead to a serious loss of morale.
>
> The right of appeal would retard the speedy punishment of those found guilty of offences of such a dastardly nature.
>
> ### Letter 216
> In WAR a soldier must cheerfully subject himself to hunger, thirst, physical and mental exhaustion and must loyally and promptly obey an order, even though knowing that the execution of that order may not only demand from him suffering, the loss of a limb, but even

of the greatest sacrifice his country can demand, THAT OF HIS OWN LIFE.

Now the present British system of Military Discipline has been so successful in training the British Soldier to this high ideal that for hundreds of years past the British Infantry (as an example) have been famous and secretly envied by foreign powers for their courage and tenacity in battle, their cohesion and refusal to accept defeat when outnumbered or in retreat and for the fact that, as they invariably turn out the 'BETTER STAYERS', they emerge triumphant in the end . . .

Germany, that proud nation, was forced to sue for peace owing to the INTERNAL COLLAPSE OF DISCIPLINE IN HER ARMY AND NAVY. In her Army the most disgraceful scenes of indiscipline occurred, of a nature that could not be contemplated in ours, until all military cohesion and will to fight disappeared. If my memory serves me right, both those two master-craftsmen of the art of war, Field Marshal von Hindenburg and his Quartermaster General, Ludendorff, attributed a major part of the disaster to the fact that the German Government introduced civil restrictions into the Military law and used this as a wedge to finally remove or restrict the powers of punishment previously held by Military Commanders.

On the other hand, our British Army, though starting with every disadvantage, and suffering terribly whilst building itself up to some four million strength from a few hundred thousand, thanks to our existing system of military discipline, wise, tolerant, just, swift, but SELF-CONTAINED, emerged triumphant.[6]

Letter 57
The less we have of civilian interference with the internal affairs of our Services, the better. The services can mind their own business without the assistance of civilian 'gold diggers'.

I speak from experience. The officer of today is just as fine a man, and a gentleman, as the officer of days gone by. I have often heard men say that they would prefer to be tried by Court Martial rather than by civilian court. They would receive fair play and justice on the evidence given, but not on what lawyers and solicitors offered as 'evidence', confusing both magistrate and Judge, and the jury.

My suggestion, if I may give it: Keep clear of all civilian interference, be it never so 'wise', legal 'gold diggers', pacifists, mischievous agitators and others, the enemies, conscious and unconscious (being mentally anaemic) of the [most] finished instrument for justice and fair play the world has ever seen – particularly in these days of cultured, civilized and unscrupulous thought and action – to wit, the Services, combatant and non-combatant, of England, clean and straight.[7]

Many strongly held the opposite view; here are some of their letters:

Letter 96
When a soldier is arrested under the Army Act, it is almost certain that he can be proved guilty of something and further evidence against him, if existent, is collected easily in a unit. The arresting NCO, the prosecutor, the court and ultimately the gaoler are, in the prisoner's mind, all in league against him and, where every man has learned of the 'democracy' of King John's barons, there must be a general feeling in the ranks that a soldier accused of a crime has not a fair chance . . . .

Hundreds of RFC officers went to France every month without any knowledge of military law and without any means of acquiring a knowledge.[8]

Letter 205
During the war five men of our Division were shot, two of them mere boys, under 19 years of age. Their field-conduct sheets were satisfactory, I remember, and the several defences were the same – i.e. 'Wind Up'. As the

proceedings passed through the customary channel from GOC to GOC, I observed no recommendation on account of youth. In fact, on the whole, general officers seemed fairly partial to the infliction of the penalty, and made no effort for commutation, even though the C in C on many occasions commuted the sentence in spite of this.[9]

Letter 11
The majority of the troops are perfectly satisfied with the present system of trial by Courts Martial, except for the method of 'prisoner's friend' [legal/solicitor used]; if not the only alternative is an officer of the Regiment, generally a junior subaltern, who is considered to have no chance against the prosecutor, who is invariably the Adjutant.

Any method of appeal to a civil judicial tribunal is against a soldier's principle.

Letter 93
The mischief, I suggest, is caused by the amateur status of the members of the Court Martial, almost invariably young and inexperienced men who are very much influenced by the attitude of the President.[10]

Letter 378
Where the accused is represented by a 'Friend' and not an officer, it is suggested that the 'Friend of the accused' should have the same rights as a Defending Officer, as regards examination and cross-examination of witnesses and addressing the court. Under the existing procedure this is debarred and it is considered that the friend of the accused might possibly be restricted in his efforts owing to the low mentality, bad enunciation, etc, of the man he is defending, especially with regards to questions to witnesses, addressing the court, etc.[11]

Letter 12a

[The writer of this letter was in favour of the right to appeal.]

The ground on which the thesis is based is not that the writer has observed any unfairness or irregularities – but rather as a necessary safeguard against what might happen.

The chief point in postulating appeal is the death sentence in time of war. Let it be said at once that the right to shoot down a man, or body of men, fleeing in the face of the enemy must be rigidly preserved. The present writer stopped the flight of a whole regiment (not his own) by covering them with Lewis guns and threatening to open fire, if they did not stop. He further secured the Distinguished Conduct Medal for one of his sergeants, who shot down one of his own officers, who ran towards the enemy, with his hands up in surrender.

But at a Court Martial, where an immediate effect on morale is not necessary, one ought to remember that human life is a precious thing and, in time of war, that is just what one forgets. The members of the court are themselves facing death day by day, they see men killed all round them: the feeling of Regimental pride and tradition . . .

One cannot weigh evidence properly under conditions of active service. No one is quite normal, and human life is held cheaply.[12]

A prefatory note by the Secretaries of State for War and Air stated that the report vindicated in general the existing court-martial system, and did not favour any change whereby a person convicted by court martial would be given a right to appeal to a civil judicial tribunal. It made a number of recommendations relating to the status and office of the Judge Advocate General. However, paragraph 8 read:

In as much as the object of the Committee was to discover if possible where the system had failed, in every case where complaint was made of injustice resulting from any trial by Court Martial, no matter how long ago, we invited the complainant to attend personally before us with a view to testing the nature and substance of his complaint, at the same time informing him that we could not act as a Court of Appeal. The total of such cases was 17, ranging in date from the year 1917 to the present time, an average of less than one a year. In every case the transcripts and records of the Proceedings were before the Committee. The Chairman personally studied the whole of these Proceedings and was satisfied, as were the Committee, that not one of them disclosed any miscarriage of justice. In making this statement it must be understood that the Committee is not expressing any opinion as to the truthfulness of the evidence in any case. That was, of course, a matter for the Tribunal in each case. We concerned ourselves only to see that there was in every case proper evidence on which the Court Martial, properly directed, could and did act.

The Committee consider that the facts stated in the last paragraph constitute the best answer to the critics of the present Court-Martial system, and furnish a very great tribute not only to the system as a whole but to the ability and care exercised in the Office of the Judge Advocate General. We cannot sufficiently emphasize the importance of the result that our studied search for cases of injustice covering a period of 20 years, and from all over the world, has discovered not a single one.[13]

The Oliver Committee report was to be followed by the Interdepartmental Courts-Martial Committee 1939. This was constituted to consider its recommendations. It sat under the Chairmanship of Sir Henry MacGeagh KBE TD KC, the Judge Advocate General of the Forces.[14]

And the present day? There is now a statutory right of appeal, since the introduction of the Courts-Martial (Appeals) Act 1951, which was amended in 1968. Members of all three services can appeal to the Courts-Martial Court, which is the Court of Appeal (Criminal Division) in another jurisdiction. The right applies only as to finding, that is guilt or innocence, and not as to sentence although the Courts-Martial Appeals Court has the power to reduce the sentence, if it quashes the finding of some but not all the charges. The appellant must first petition the Defence Council and the right is exercisable only if they reject his petition. He must then obtain leave to appeal from the Courts-Martial Appeal Court itself. This is usually given by a single judge.[15]

References

1. House of Lords, Record Office: HC Sessional Papers 1924–5, IX: Report of the Interdepartmental Committee on Proposed Disciplinary Amendments of the Army and Air Force Acts 1925.
2. House of Lords, Record Office: Parliamentary Debates, (237) Commons (1930), cc 1567–1630.
3. House of Lords, Record Office: Parliamentary Debates, (77) Lords (1929–1930), 15 April 1930.
4. House of Lords, Record Office: Parliamentary Debates, (237) Commons (1930), 16 April 1930.
5. Public Record Office, Kew, ref. WO 225/9: The Army and Air Force Courts-Martial Committee, 29 March 1938 (Oliver Committee).
6. Public Record Office, Kew, ref. WO 225/2: Letters laid before Committee. Letters 204–517.
7. Public Record Office, Kew, ref. WO 225/15: Incoming Letters 36–97.
8. Public Record Office, Kew, ref. WO 225/1: Letters laid before Committee. Letters 1–203.
9. Public Record Office, Kew, ref. WO 225/2: Letters laid before Committee. Letters 204–517.
10. Public Record Office, Kew, ref. WO 225/1: Letters laid before Committee. Letters 1–203.
11. Public Record Office, Kew, ref. WO 225/2: Letters laid before Committee. Letters 204–517.

12. Public Record Office, Kew, ref. WO 224[14]: Letter Book. 1–35.
13. Public Record Office, Kew, ref. WO 225/9: Report of Committee.
14. Public Record Office, Kew, ref. WO 225/10: Interdepartmental Courts-Martial Committee 1939: To Secretaries of State for War and Air.
15. Letter to L.G. Sellers of 10 November 1993 from Chief Naval Judge Advocate, Royal Naval College, Greenwich, ref. CNJA 689.

CHAPTER TEN

Fair or Foul

Fair or foul – emotive words. In this chapter the intention is to try and find the answer to the basic question: Did Edwin Dyett receive justice? Or were the dice so loaded in favour of the prosecution that he had little chance of an adequate defence?

Sometimes in life situations develop when an individual becomes a pawn to be sacrificed for the common good. Before the court came a young, single and inexperienced junior officer, who fully realized his own limitations, as he had made four applications for transfer. He was described by his Commanding Officer as being a poor officer and having little authority to command men. Furthermore, he was an officer of the 63rd (RN) Division – not one of the regular Army divisions, but naval reservists and marines who did not conform to Army ways and nomenclature, resistant to change, dragged kicking and screaming into line, but still holding fast to its naval traditions; a division that had recently lost its guiding hand and father figure, Major-General Sir Archibald Paris, who had been replaced by Major-General Cameron Deane Shute, a man with a very low regard for his new charges. For an officer of Shute's background to be OC of a naval unit must have been a strange and stressful experience. He set about finding fault in all directions so that an antipathy grew up between him and the old guard of officers and men alike. Indeed, some-times army officers were brought in over the heads of more senior naval reserve officers. This was very irritating to the more free-minded and intelligent RND officer. Basil Rackham of the Hawke Battalion and A.P. Herbert's assistant adjutant states that, when a regular army commanding officer was imposed on them – a very decent fellow, but slow-witted and unintelligent – A.P. Herbert found it very irksome.[1]

It is clear that Shute's attitude and the General Staff's opinion of the RND did not help. When an example needs to be made, one naturally looks to the outsider ('Not one of us'). Even after the Division's success at the Battle of the Ancre the War Office was not content. A letter of 27 December, 1916, to the Admiralty stated:

> I am commanded by the Army Council to inform you that the military efficiency of the 63rd Royal Naval Division has suffered seriously owing to the following difficulties arising from the fact that the Naval units of the Divisions are administered partly on a Naval, and partly on a Military basis.[2]

A clue can be found in entries in Field Marshal Haig's diaries which highlight his opinion of the Naval Division, and Admiralty units:

Monday, 6th November 1916
In the afternoon I inspected a squadron of naval aeroplanes lent me by the Admiralty. I rode to Vert Gallant. The aeroplanes are mostly Sopwiths and are quite new. The commander seemed to be the only sailor in the whole show. Even the 'ship's cook', as he was called, in reply to my questions regarding his services at sea, replied that he was a soldier transferred for the purpose of cooking.[3]

Wednesday, 13th December 1916
I have written War Office recommending that the Naval Division be transferred to a Military organization. At present the div is partly administered by Admiralty and partly by War Office. As regards the part administered

143

by the former, out of the 6 RNR Battalions there is not a single Naval officer and only one (a retired Lieutenant) who has ever been in the Navy. There are only 19 serving officers of the Royal Marines and ten of these have been promoted from the ranks since the war. The others are New Army Officers (except 2 COs). The case is the same as regards the men. There are no real sailors and very few marines. The personnel is of lower quality than that in the New Army, but they all receive more pay.[4]

The Army Council set out a number of problems and grievances. On 8 February, 1917, a conference was held in Committee Room 13, at the House of Commons. The Admiralty was represented by the First Lord of the Admiralty, The Right Hon. Sir Edward Carson KC MP. Carson remarked on the lack of sympathy of the General Officer Commanding, and the fact that officers had been brought in over the heads of their seniors in the Naval Battalion, and also in the Royal Marines. On 7 March the War Office gave in; the problems of a complete transfer were too great.[5] A compromise was reached but it was always a relationship of opposites.

As I wrote in my history of the Hood Battalion:

Once more the RND had survived, but it had been a hard fight which was to prove to be only a battle won, not the war. However, one matter of grievance was overcome when Major-General Shute was succeeded on the 19th February by Major General C.E. Lawrie DSO. This was only 11 days after the conference. The Division still had some political clout and friends in high places, and in the traditions of the Navy was not going to sink without a struggle.[6]

But why execute Dyett, when countless other officers of both junior and more senior rank must have failed, shown cowardice and committed a capital offence? During the First World War only three officers were executed. On 24 September 1918 a 2nd Lieutenant of the 3rd Essex was shot for murder. This example can therefore be disregarded, as it has little bearing on Dyett's case. So there was only one other unfortunate. On 10 December, 1916, 2nd Lieutenant E.S. Poole of the 11th West Yorks was executed for desertion. It is strange that during 1914, 1915 and most of 1916 there were no other executions of officers[7] – or any others during the rest of the war. We have a paradox. Why in late 1916 were examples needed? Why was a blood-letting required? Why was Dyett expendable?

Field Marshal Haig made an entry in his diary of Wednesday, 6 December, 1916, concerning 2nd Lieutenant E.S. Poole which is a very useful indication as to his thinking at that time:

> This morning the AG brought me Court-Martial proceedings on an officer charged with desertion and sentenced by the Court to be shot. After careful consideration I confirmed the proceedings. This is the first sentence of death on an officer to be put into execution since I became C-in-C. Such a crime is more serious in the case of an officer than of a man, and also it is highly important that all ranks should realize that the law is the same for an officer as a private.[8]

But there are additional factors which might have had an influence on Dyett's fate. The first is that an example was required, as desertion had become somewhat prevalent at the time. Evidence to this effect was given in 1922 by Colonel J.F.C. Fuller DSO. At the Enquiry into Shell Shock he stated:

> If a crowd of men are reduced to a low nervous condition, 'shell-shock', so-called, becomes contagious. This was noticeable at the Battle of the Ancre in 1916, the only battle in which I had direct evidence that British troops deserted in considerable numbers to the enemy. I believe that this was due to the low nervous condition produced by the appalling surroundings of this battle.[9]

The second was that in particular the 189th Brigade of the 63rd (RN) Division did so well at this battle, and the Hood Battalion under the inspired leadership of its commanding officer, Bernard Freyberg, especially so. Haig was to write an entry in his diary of Monday, 20 November, 1916, as follows:

> After lunch I motored to Candas, where I was met by General Shute commanding the Naval Division. I then inspected the 189th Brigade (General Phillips) which did so well in the recent attack on Beaumont Hamel. I also saw at Frencillers Colonel Freyberg's battalion (the Hood). That officer has been recommended for the VC because when the line of attack was held up he rallied parts of three battalions and broke through the German front. But for his action, victory might not have been attained.[10]

When Haig and his staff were confronted with the two extremes, with such black and white examples – the heroism of Freyberg and Edwin Dyett's desertion (he was duty-bound to go up to the front in support of Freyberg) his crime was highlighted. He was a victim of circumstance and timing; a pawn in the wider game of war; expendable, unworthy and tainted with failure; the last officer to die for lack of backbone and moral fibre in the annals of British military history, and a naval officer to boot.

There was disquiet about the execution in the Naval Division. Basil Bedsmore Rackham MC, who was later to become a Brigadier and who had himself been wounded at the Ancre, but had remained on duty, wrote:

> I did not know Dyett personally, nor all the details of the case. But we – juniors – all felt that, had his commanding officer and others lived, Dyett's case might have been handled differently.
>
> I think I am right in saying that A.P. Herbert was asked to act as 'Prisoner's Friend', but declined.
>
> Another unfortunate aspect of the case was that the

principal witness for the prosecution was a most unpopular officer.

Rackham continued:

> After the Ancre A.P. Herbert became Adjutant and I was his assistant, till April, 1917, when he was wounded and invalided home. During this time, incensed by what he considered to be the injustice of the Dyett case and maybe others, he often spoke of the possibility of writing a book about Courts Martial.[11]

In 1919 A.P. Herbert wrote *The Secret Battle*, which contained an introduction by Winston Churchill.[12] It is the story of Harry Penrose, a junior officer. The story outlines his time at Gallipoli and on the Western Front. He also comes up against an old enemy and dies at dawn. It is a story of much pathos and depth and was written from the heart. Reginald Pound, the author of A.P. Herbert's biography, wrote in 1980 that: 'I think there is no doubt whatever that *The Secret Battle* was written as an emotional discharge arising out of the court martial . . . I have no doubt either that APH would not have been spurred to write a novel on such a theme otherwise.'[13]

But what of the court-martial file? what can one learn? It contains no summary of evidence. When in 1918 the Under Secretary for War said, concerning the summary of evidence, 'I am almost certain that he had, because I believe it is the law that the accused person must have it, in any case he must have known the evidence against him!'[14], he could not say otherwise, as it is missing. But why?
The Manual of Military Law, v 28, paragraph 604 states:

> When making application to a convening officer for a district or general court martial the commanding officer forwards with it the charge sheet, summary of evidence, company conduct sheets, list of witnesses to be called, and a statement as to character and particulars of

service of the accused. A surgeon's certificate as to the ability of the accused to undergo imprisonment is appended.[15]

Now this summary of evidence was very important, as King's Regulation 59 stated when dealing with the duties of President:

> During the trial he should compare the evidence by the witnesses with the summary of evidence, and if there by any material different he should question the witnesses about it.[16]

How is it that no summary can be found? During my research at the Public Record Office at Kew, I found no summary in any file that I examined. Now, if the President of a Court Martial should have detached or have had with him this summary for his use during the hearing, it seems unlikely that in all these cases it would not have been put back with the main file, once the court martial was concluded. In any case, if there were no summary, how in all honesty could the Judge Advocate, whose duty it was to check the legality of the court martial, do so without it?

There is another matter that needs to be aired. This is the question of a medical examination before the trial. King's Regulations, paragraph 580 stated:

> Soldiers ordered for trial are to be examined by a medical officer on the morning of each day that the court is ordered to sit, and commanding officer will be held responsible that no soldier is brought before a court martial if in the opinion of the medical officer he is unfit to undergo his trial.[17]

When I examined the court-martial file of Edwin Dyett I could find no reference to the fact that he had undergone such an examination and as a result was fit to stand trial.[18] I therefore decided to examine at random six other court-martial files held at the Public Record Office. What I found was very informative and highlights the concern that a great number of men who were executed did not receive justice.

Ref. WO 71/509): Private Harry Farr, 1st Battalion, West Yorkshire Regiment. Cowardice. Executed 18 October, 1916

I found the following declaration and certificate as required in King's Regulations, paragraph 580:

> I certify that I examined No 887 Pt H. Farr 1st West Yorks on Oct 2nd 1916 and that in my opinion both his general physical and mental condition were satisfactory.
> W. Williams, MO

> *Certificate*
> 8871 Pte FARR   I certify that the marginally named man is fit to undergo the strain of trial by Field General Court Martial
> W. Williams, Captain RAMC
> MO i/c 1st Battalion,
> West Yorkshire Regiment

This certificate was counter-signed by Lieut.-Col. F. Spring, 11th Essex Regt, President of Court Martial, 2 October, 1916.[19]

However, when I examined the other five files (WO 71/529, WO 71/552, WO 71/514, WO 71/520 and WO 71/422)[20], as with Edwin Dyett's, there is no evidence that King's Regulation 580 had been complied with; there were no declarations, no certificates. Indeed, there were statements that no medical examination had been made before trial, while requests for them were to be made after conviction but before confirmation. One file is a terrible indictment as it is clear that a knowledge of the prisoner's mental and medical condition was very relevant to the case. In WO 71/422 (the court-martial file of Rifleman W. Ballamy 1/KRRC, who was executed for cowardice on 16 July 1915) I found that an examination was asked for after the trial but not before, and the following report, on behalf of a lieutenant-general:

> I am doubtful whether the evidence as recorded is sufficient to legally sustain conviction on a charge of cowardice.

In consequence it was found necessary to issue notes on guidance for officers taking evidence so that this did not take place again. The evidence was taken down incorrectly, but still it was decided that Ballamy could pay the ultimate price.

From these examples one must ask: Where is the justice here? the rule of law? the protection for the weak in body and mind? Some of the checks and balances of even-handed justice were lost by lack of knowledge and care in the bigger challenge of winning the war. The total propriety, impartiality and legitimacy of many courts-martial can be questioned – a blemish on our history and ethics.

Now I come to another strange circumstance. During my research I wanted to obtain a copy of Edwin Dyett's death certificate. So in August, 1993, I visited St Katherine's House in London. I found the entry in the Naval War Records of Deaths 1914–1921. But to my surprise his entry had been an afterthought, entered in ink, and out of order in the margin. My astonishment grew when, upon receiving the copy of the certificate by post, I found that the cause of death had been given as 'On War Service'.[21] Other such death certificates state that the person was executed; why not Dyett?

I therefore wrote to the General Register Office at Southport, asking for clarification as to why his entry had been missed out originally and what was the reason for not showing the cause of death. Was Dyett given a pardon? I was aware that, after hearing of the execution, his father had started a campaign to have his son's name cleared.[22] The reply was that death registrations made for the First World War were authorized and registered by the

Ministry of Defence; there was nothing unusual about this particular entry; Dyett's actual cause of death was not shown, as the GRO had been instructed by the MoD to show the cause of death as it appears on the death certificate.[23] Following up[24], I was told that the entry was inserted into the records in 1989 on the authority of the MoD as it had been found to be missing by a member of the public. The GRO staff did not know why they were instructed to show the wording as given.[25]

By November the MoD informed me that they had advised the Registrar General's Office of the necessary details and asked them to register Dyett's death. The cause of death was to be recorded as 'Shot by order of General Court Martial for desertion at St Firmin, France'. They did not know why, nor would they be able to establish why the death was not registered at the time of death. They had no knowledge of Commander Dyett's efforts to clear his son's name.[26]

With that I gave up; I was knocking my head against a brick wall. Still, strangely, fate has taken a hand. Dyett is shown as having died 'On War Service'. It is an epitaph which is fitting for a volunteer who was not a leader of men, but who died most gallantly.

References

1. Rackham, Basil, letter to Judge Anthony Babington of 31 March, 1980.
2. Public Record Office, Kew, ref. ADM1 8477/309.
3. Public Record Office, Kew, ref. WO 256/14: Haig's Diaries, entry of Monday, 6 November, 1916.
4. Public Record Office, Kew, ref. WO 256/14: Haig's Diaries, entry of Wednesday, 13 December, 1916.
5. Public Record Office, Kew, ref. ADM 1/309.
6. Sellers, Leonard, *The Hood Battalion*, Leo Cooper, 1994.
7. Putkowski, Julian and Sykes, Julian, *Shot at Dawn*, Leo Cooper, revised ed. 1992.
8. Public Record Office, Kew, ref. WO 256/14: Haig's

Diaries, entry of Wednesday, 6 December, 1916.

9. House of Lords, Record Office: Report on War Office Committee of Enquiry into 'Shell Shock' 1922, HC Sessional Papers, Accounts & Papers 2, XII, 1922, p. 788.

10. Public Record Office, Kew, ref. WO 256/14: Haig's Diaries, entry of Monday, 20 November, 1916.

11. Rackham, Basil, letter to Judge Anthony Babington of 15 March, 1980, pp 2 & 3.

12. Herbert, A.P., *The Secret Battle*, Methuen, 1919.

13. Pound, Anthony, letter to Judge Anthony Babington of 23 February, 1980.

14. House of Lords, Records Office, HC Deb, 5th Series (14 March, 1918), Vol I, cc 562–72.

15. Pratt, Sisson C., Lieut-Col. RA, Military Handbook *Military Law*, Kegan Paul, Trench Trubner, 1910, Chapter IX p. 66.

16. Pratt, Sisson C. S66 Duties of President. Chapter VII, p. 55.

17. Pratt, Sisson C. S85 The Accused. Chapter IX. p. 75.

18. Public Record Office, Kew, ref. ADM 156/24.

19. Public Record Office, Kew, ref. WO 71/509.

20. Public Record Office, Kew, refs
WO 71/529: Private 5009 S. McBride, 2nd Royal Irish Rifles
WO 71/552: Private W. Robinson, 1st Sherwood Foresters
WO 71/514: Private Harry McDonald, 12th Battalion, West Yorkshire Regiment
WO 71/520: L/Cpl William Arthur Moon, 11th Battalion, Cheshire Regiment
WO 71/422: Rifleman No 3319 W. Ballamy, 1/KRRC

21. General Register Office, ref. SA 047023: death certificate of Edwin Leopold Arthur Dyett, (application no. PSR G 004879).

22. Sellers, Leonard George, letter of 25 August, 1993, to General Register Office, Southport.

23. Office of Population Censuses & Surveys, ref. PSRG 004879: letter to L.G. Sellers of 8 September, 1993.

24. Sellers, L.G., letter of 9 September, 1993, Office of Population Censuses & Surveys, Southport.
25. OPCS, ref. PSRG 004979: letter to L.G. Sellers of 16 September 1993.
26. Ministry of Defence, Old Admiralty Building, ref. D/NPC/89/3: letter of L.G. Sellers 8 November, 1993.

CHAPTER ELEVEN

I Cannot Change History

In 1917 the Admiralty reviewed a number of court-martial files relating to officers. In Dyett's court-martial file, dated 1 June, 1917, under the heading 'Submission and Minutes', can be found the following:

> Submitted for information. These minutes are sent to Admiralty in order that the Admiralty in exceptional cases be able to exercise their right to reduce sentence, also for the purpose of record. It was recognized that this was impracticable when the death penalty is awarded as here in Lieutenant Dyett's case.[1]

But, as we have seen, the matter would not rest. Uneasy stirrings broke the surface from time to time, held down only by lack of knowledge, secrecy and obstruction. Discontent, disturbed feelings and a restless search for the truth were to grow with the thought that some of the 307 soldiers executed had been harshly treated. In 1974 William Moore published *The Thin Yellow Line*. It asked questions and gave some answers, but was hampered by lack of available official papers.[2] Then Judge Anthony Babington was allowed to research the court-martial files, the first time anyone from outside Whitehall had been given such a privilege. He published *For the Sake of Example* in 1983. He did not name individuals, but his work was a revelation and highlighted the lack of justice done in a number of cases. Coming from a man who, as a barrister, had frequently defended at overseas court martial, this must be taken as an indictment.[3] In 1989 Julian Putkowski and Julian Sykes published *Shot at Dawn* which lists and names all the men executed.[4] A head of steam was building up, as interest grew, not only within families, with historians, and in the press, but with Members of Parliament too.

During The Royal British Legion's conference of 1985 the following resolution was passed:

> This conference requests the National Executive Council to urge the Government to reopen all the 'Verdict of guilt' cases for acts of cowardice in the First World War in the light of modern medical evidence.

The Legion outlined to members the reply received:

> The reply received from the Under-Secretary of State at the Ministry of Defence to the representations made by your Council on the terms of this Resolution explained that the Government accepted that a number of men who were executed for cowardice at that time might now, in the light of modern psychiatric knowledge, be judged to have been suffering from battle exhaustion or battle shock, and not therefore fully responsible for their actions. Although their sentences were in accordance with the law and conditions of the time, the under-standing of battle stress has moved on since then, and this was recognized by the decision to abolish the death penalty for cases of this kind before the Second World War.
>
> A review of individual cases would however be impracticable. Even if the resolution was read in its nar-rowest sense, i.e. as referring to the 18 or so cases of executions for cowardice, it was most unlikely that conclusive assessments could be made because of the paucity of medical evidence and because, in psychiatric conditions of this kind, a diagnosis can often only be made after lengthy interviews and tests with the partic-ular individual. The medical view is that no meaningful

reappraisal could be made after so many years.

Whilst this consideration was crucial, it should be added that, if the resolution were read in its literal sense – i.e. a review of all those convicted of cowardice, or of other offences in which cowardice played a part, irrespective of whether the death penalty or some lesser punishment were awarded – then it is unlikely that the necessary records still exist on which to base such a review. The proceedings of trials in which the death sentence was not awarded or put into effect have not been retained and many personal records of the period were destroyed by enemy action in 1940.

The minister sympathized with those who felt that injustices were done during World War I, but it would be equally unjust to those who fought and died gallantly in equally appalling conditions to give a general exoneration to those convicted of cowardice at the time, much though the attitude of the authorities to the offence has changed in the interim.

Your Council having considered the terms of the reply were of the opinion that no useful purpose would be served by pursuing this issue.[5]

On 15 June, 1992, ten Members of Parliament, headed by Andrew Mackinlay MP, introduced a Notice of Motions:

That this House believes it is not too late to restore the names and reputation of the 307 soldiers of the British Empire Forces court-martialled and executed, mostly on the Western Front, in the four years 1914–1918, following charges ranging from desertion, cowardice, quitting posts, sleeping at posts, disobedience, striking a superior officer and casting away arms; regrets deficiencies in their opportunity to prepare adequate defence and appeals; notes the marked and enlightened change in the Army's attitude just over a score years later to the consequences of soldiers enduring long periods of severe cold and damp, lack of food and sleep coupled with the stress and shock of constant shell fire with the result that not a single soldier was executed on these charges throughout the six years from 1939 to 1945; considers that the vast majority of the 307 executed were as patriotic and brave as their million other compatriots who perished in the conflict and that their misfortune was brought about due to stress, or the stress of their accusers, during battle and, even if the behaviour of a small minority may have fallen below that of the highest standards, then time, compassion and justice dictates that all of these soldiers should now be treated as victims of the conflict; and urges the Prime Minister to recommend a posthumous pardon for all 307, thus bringing to a close a deeply unhappy and controversial chapter in the history of the Great War.[6]

Andrew Mackinlay, the Labour MP for Thurrock, then began his campaign in earnest to obtain pardons for the executed. This elicited a letter from John Major, the Prime Minister, on 16 July, 1992, in which he mentioned a proposed meeting between Mackinlay and Lord Cranborne, the Parliamentary Under-Secretary of State for Defence, to discuss the implications. As a result of this meeting Cranborne set in motion an examination of a number of files of executed servicemen to establish exactly what documentation was available and, as far as possible, whether the proper procedures had been followed.[7] On 10 February, 1993, the Prime Minister wrote again, saying:

10 February 1993

Dear Andrew,
Following our earlier correspondence about British soldiers who were executed during the First World War, I am now able to reply fully. As you know, I have been waiting to see the outcome of the researches which Robert Cranborne set in hand after you met him. He has considered this distressing matter with great care and I have now been able to consider his conclusions.

We have had a sample of some thirty files in the Public Record Office examined, constituting about ten per cent of the cases which concern you. The sample included files open to the public and some still closed.

It seems to me that there are two main grounds on which pardons might be recommended.

The first is that of legal impropriety or procedural error. The files record each stage of the case, up to the final decision by the Commander-in-Chief. No evidence was found to lead us, including the Judge Advocate General, to think that the convictions were unsound or that the accused were treated unfairly at the time.

The second ground is humanitarian. I accept that this is a much more difficult area. I appreciate the distress which surviving relatives of the soldiers concerned, such as Mrs Farr, still feel. And I greatly sympathize with them. I do think it essential, however, that full account is taken of the circumstances of the time.

The First World War was probably the bloodiest conflict ever. At certain periods, troops from this country and those of our Allies were being killed at a rate of tens of thousands a day. Soldiers who deserted were sentenced against this background of heavy casualties amongst the vast majority of their fellow soldiers who were carrying out orders. The authorities at the time took the view that deserters had to receive due punishment because of the effect of desertions on the military capacity and morale of the Allied armies. Millions of soldiers put their lives at risk and endured the most terrible sufferings. They had to be able to rely on the support of their comrades in arms.

As to shell-shock and the stress of mind of the soldiers concerned, medical evidence is not always available on each file and, in many cases, was not a factor in the soldier's plea of mitigation. However, shell-shock did become recognized as a medical condition during the First World War. And, where medical evidence was available to the court, it was taken into account in sentencing and in the recommendations on the final sentence made to the Commander-in-Chief.

Most death sentences were commuted on the basis of medical evidence.

I have reflected long and hard but I have reached the conclusion that we cannot re-write history by substituting our latter-day judgment for that of contemporaries, whatever we might think. With the passage of time, attitudes and values change. This applies as much to past civilian trials as to military ones, in which sentences were imposed based on the values of the time. I am sure that all people, when they think of this subject now, recognize that those soldiers who deserted did so in the most appalling conditions and under terrible pressures and take that fully into account in reaching any judgment in their own mind.

You mentioned allegations by Robert Graves, and the Canadian Government's pardon of their executed soldiers. I have had those examined and no evidence has been found to confirm the allegation made by Graves that a 'secret order' was issued, instructing officers that instances of cowardice were to be punished by the death sentence.

The Canadian authorities have provided written confirmation to the Ministry of Defence that there is no evidence that a pardon for the Canadian soldiers concerned has ever been granted or considered.

I am very sorry to send what I know will be a deeply disappointing reply, disappointing not only to you but to the surviving relatives of the soldiers who were executed. Colleagues and I have looked at this very carefully indeed and we have not lightly come to our decision.

Yours sincerely
John Major[8]

This letter troubles me. Note the Prime Minister's sentence, 'Most death sentences were commuted on the basis of medical evidence'. No doubt he was being briefed by the Under-Secretary of State for Defence, but I refer the reader to the British Legion's conference resolution back in 1985.

The then Under-Secretary of State for Defence replied that 'The proceedings of trials in which the death sentence was not awarded or put into effect *have not been retained*' (my italics).[9] Indeed later, in the House of Lords debate of 4 November, 1993, Lord Cranborne stated: 'The files of the soldiers who were reprieved were burnt during an incendiary attack in 1941 on the Arnside Street repository.' How is it therefore known that '*Most death sentences were commuted on the basis of medical evidence*'? The files are gone, destroyed. Is it therefore the case that before 1941 extensive research into the matter had been undertaken? It is indeed strange that, in many of the files of men who were shot, medical evidence is sparse or non-existent, but in other cases medical evidence became the prime reason for commuting the sentence.

Andrew Mackinlay wrote again to the Prime Minister:

17 Feb 93

Dear Prime Minister

With reference to your letter of 10 February, I cannot overstate how personally grateful I am for the courtesy extended to me and attention you have given to my request for British soldiers executed in the First World War to be pardoned.

However, I am disappointed that you feel unable to substantially revise the perspective which has been expressed by Ministry of Defence on this issue.

With regard to the research carried out on a sample of thirty cases in the Public Record Office, I would be grateful if you could arrange for the relevant department to let me know a few further details about the scope of research and findings.

I am interested to know the basis on which the sample was determined and compiled. I would also like to know the ages, names and ranks of the executed men; the specific offences for which they were sentenced; their length of service and previous disciplinary record; whether they were provided with a defending officer; whether evidence was presented, either to the court or the confirming officers, about the accused's previous medical record.

Your affirmation that the convictions were sound and the accused were treated fairly clearly does not accord with evidence drawn from cases which have been made public. The views of the Judge Advocate General concerning the legality and procedural rectitude of these trials were not unexpected, but I cannot agree with your contention that the accused were treated fairly at the time. At an elementary level, for example, the accused should have been advised they had the right to lodge a personal appeal for a pardon from HM the King. There is no evidence to show they were so informed.

I similarly find it impossible to accept the reasons advanced for refusing a pardon on humanitarian grounds. There is no evidence, statistical or otherwise, to indicate there was a link between the confirmation of death sentences and any measurable improvement in military capacity and morale. No death sentences were confirmed on Australian troops who were found guilty of capital offences, and neither their morale nor behaviour in combat was ever in doubt. If anything, there is contemporary testimony that executions had an adverse effect on unit morale.

From cases which I have examined, I believe it is correct to maintain that references to shell-shock, or post-traumatic stress disorder, do not always feature in medical evidence or soldiers' pleas in mitigation. It is, however, incorrect to assume that the court or confirming authorities, on any but the most haphazard basis, took a man's medical record into account in their deliberations. In fact, there are regrettable examples where it is clear that medical evidence of battle stress was submitted and excluded from consideration by the authorities. It was not unusual, especially in the latter part of the war, for a medical officer to affirm that a man was medically fit to be tried. However, I am unable to cite a single case in which any confirming officer commented on the medical record of the accused. In many cases officers stated no reason for confirming the sentence of the court and merely appended their signatures to the schedule.

It is a pleasure to agree with your conclusion that it is not possible to re-write history. However, it has not been possible for historians to examine in detail these tragic affairs precisely because, until now, individual case files have been withheld, and in some cases continue to be withheld, from scrutiny by Parliament and the public.

I feel heartened by your acknowledgement that, with the passage of time, attitudes and values change, but compassion for the frailties of one's fellow men and their families is not yet outmoded. Please could I request that you exercise this quality, thereby making tangible a measure to personally endorse universal recognition of the appalling conditions and terrible pressures which caused soldiers' nerves to break.

Also accept my thanks for checking the allegations that the Canadian authorities had pardoned their executed soldiers and the apparent misunderstanding of Robert Graves. That both reports prove to be unfounded is scant comfort to these, in Canada and elsewhere, whose menfolk, like Pte Harry Farr, were executed for cowardice.

Pte Farr, a verbatim transcript of whose brief trial is recorded in the papers I enclose, was acknowledged to have had shell-shock but was still executed for cowardice. His family have endured undeserved years of harrowing emotional distress as a consequence of the confirming authorities' decision to ignore the report of Farr's medical condition. On behalf of Farr's elderly widow and surviving family, and as representative example of the other cases with which I am concerned, I ask that you reconsider your rejection of my request for a pardon.

Your sincerely
Andrew Mackinlay[10]

The Prime Minister replied:

Dear Andrew

Thank you for your letter of 17 February about soldiers executed during the First World War. I am sorry that I have not replied before now but, once again, Robert Cranborne and I have been giving this very careful consideration.

I quite understand your wish to establish the basis on which the files were researched. The sample of 30 files was chosen to span the entire period of the First World War but was otherwise entirely a random selection. The researchers were not aware of the individual circumstances of each case prior to the files being examined.

The remaining files, currently closed under Section 5 (1) of the Public Records Acts 1958 and 1967, are being released on a rolling basis. Those closed in 1917 were made available for public examination in January; those for 1918 are due for release in 1994.

Your questions about age, rank, specific offences and other detailed matters will require a little time to answer. Some points were not recorded separately by the Ministry of Defence in examining the files, which have now been returned to the Public Record Office. Clarification may take some time but the Ministry of Defence will let you have the details as soon as possible.

The effect of executions on soldiers' morale is bound to be a matter of debate amongst contemporary historians and was bound to be so among observers at the time. They were, however, firmly felt to be necessary by those in positions of command during the war. It is possible to reach different judgments, especially with the benefit of hindsight. But to argue that this means pardons should now be granted would result in the alteration of history to suit modern attitudes, a philosophy which neither you nor I subscribe to.

Your comment that Australian troops were not subject to execution is indeed correct. In response to your point about Australians' morale and behaviour being unaffected, there is evidence to suggest that the Commanders for the Australian Divisions wanted the death penalty to be enforced, believing that the discipline of Australian troops would suffer in the absence of this ultimate sanction. The Australian General Officer Commanding in France believed that, without the death penalty, the discipline of Australian troops would suffer when the men realized that they were not on precisely the same footing as other soldiers serving in France.

I am afraid that there is little I can add to what I have already written in respect of your other points. As I have said, an examination of the files has not led us to think that the convictions were unsound or that the trials were conducted unfairly at the time. I note your concern that treatment of medical evidence may have been haphazard but I do not think it is possible for us to second-guess those who participated in the trials at this distance.

I fully recognize the feelings of the Farr family and others in a similar situation. Indeed, that has made this decision all the more difficult. I respect your deep concern on this issue. I am afraid, however, that we must continue to agree to disagree.

Yours sincerely
John[11]

Correspondence continued between the Prime Minister and Andrew Mackinlay. Undaunted, he proceeded with his Private Member's Bill to obtain pardons for those officers and men executed in the Great War, apart from those executed for murder and mutiny. At 4.12pm on 19 October, 1993, he rose to speak as follows in the House of Commons:

The Bill would facilitate the granting of pardons to 307 soldiers of the British Empire forces who fought in the Great War of 1914–18 but were executed by firing squad, having been found guilty of charges that ranged from cowardice to desertion, sleeping at post, throwing away arms and hitting a superior officer.

Many of these soldiers were young men – teenagers. They were drawn from every corner of the United Kingdom. Many were not conscripts but volunteers, and some spent not months but years in the trenches enduring constant shell-fire, sniping and lack of food and sleep in the constant wet and cold. It is hardly surprising that, in many cases, their spirit broke.

All 307 soldiers were, in my submission, denied the operation of rules of natural justice. They were not given the opportunity to prepare a defence; in many cases there was no advocacy whatever and, when there was, it was not conducted by a legally qualified person. Above all, none of the soldiers was given the opportunity to appeal against the sentence of death: invariably, they were given only 12 to 24 hours' notice before the sentence was carried out. That shows that those men have endured grave injustice, and it is time that the record was put straight.

We now know from the documents that have become available, following the crazy 75-year public records' rule, that many of those men were sick, traumatized and suffering from shell-shock. For that reason, the House should begin to put the record straight to ensure that the men are held in high national esteem.

I am motivated to bring this Bill before the House because many dependents of those men seek redress, and because there are still among us a few thousand veterans of the Great War, in the evening of their lives, to which nothing would give greater satisfaction or contentment than knowing – albeit late in the day – that their comrades in arms were finally exonerated. I was pleased to see the support in the press of my Noble Friend Lord Houghton of Sowerby, a veteran of Passchendaele, who endorses my view.

It has been suggested that I am seeking to rewrite history. I reject that. I am seeking to ensure that history is written with clarity and precision and that those things that are uncomfortable to the establishment are brought into the open.

In a few weeks' time Her Majesty the Queen, the Prime Minister and the Leader of the Opposition will be at the Cenotaph, and other right hon. Members will rightly be at their local war memorials. We attend such memorials not to remember veterans of the Crimean war, the Napoleonic wars or the Cromwellian wars, but to remember soldiers of the Great War because they are of our time.

All of us have grandfathers, fathers and uncles who were in the Great War. We have all seen, spoken, touched and loved them. That is something which cannot be ignored. They are not merely history. It is long overdue that a remedy was sought to heal the reputations of those men that were broken during the sham trials in the Great War.

My Bill provides two opinions: either to grant a blanket pardon for all 307 soldiers, which I and Lord Houghton favour, or, if that is not appropriate, that the Secretary of State be able to refer each case to a panel of High Court Judges to test whether or not there has been injustice and whether or not there should be a pardon. I cannot see what can be wrong with that, other than that some people might not like the truth coming out.

The measure is universally popular. My post bag and those of other hon. Members show overwhelming public support for it. I shall go further: the difference between now and 18 months ago, when the pardons' campaign began, is that, we now know that, in a sense, the soldiers have already been pardoned by the highest court in the land – British public opinion. My Bill would facilitate an official way in which the nation could collectively say sorry.

My Bill could be a matter of national pride for our generation and this House of Commons. We could draw a line under the unhappy events of the First World War, do all we can to repair the damage done to the reputation of those men, to heal the wounds of the families and to allow the veterans of the Great War who are still alive to go to sleep tonight content in the knowledge that their comrades are now deemed to be brave soldiers.

I ask nothing more than for the opportunity for these cases to be tested by the normal criteria that operate in the land. Have the rules of national justice been applied? Were those men sick and traumatized, as I believe they were? My Bill would facilitate a test by which their cases would be put before a High Court Judge. The documents are now available and they speak for themselves.

The demand for this remedy is like a cry from the grave. It is time that the House of Commons took hold of the matter, put aside the objections of the establishment and said that those soldiers of the Great War who were executed are deemed worthy to be among those we will remember on Remembrance Sunday.

Mr Roger Evans, the MP for Monmouth, rose in reply:

The speech of the hon. Member for Thurrock [Mr A. Mackinlay] was plausible and emotional, but fundamentally misconceived and wrong in principle. History is littered with injustice, and it is entirely inappropriate at this stage in the century to examine what happened between 1914 and 1918. If ever there was an argument against open government and in favour of keeping the files closed for even longer, it could be made now. What are we hoping to achieve by the measure?

If the scheme of the hon. Member for Thurrock is designed to give a blanket pardon, it cannot be right, as a matter of principle. It will be not an examination of the historical record, but a mere expression of opinion, without any reference to the particulars of the cases. It would be a case of wasting time with a sort of war crimes' tribunal in reverse at the end of the century. That would be a monstrous procedure and wholly wrong. The matters are for historians, not the House now.

To seek to lay blame by using the word 'establishment', as the hon. Member for Thurrock did, was an extremely unfortunate way of attacking the British state. The fact remains that we are the beneficiaries of the sacrifices made by our grandparents' generation, and it would be wholly wrong to continue with the scheme.[12]

Mr Andrew Mackinlay nevertheless presented his Bill to pardon soldiers, which was read for the first time and ordered to be read a second time on 11 November. Still there would be a long hard road to follow before it could become law and it now just sits on the table, awaiting time, that is unlikely to be granted, as has been the fate of numerous Private Members' Bills. On 1 July, 1994, Andrew Mackinlay presented to the House of Commons a petition signed by more than 25,000 people. This was also laid upon the Table in the presence of Madame Speaker and stated:

> Wherefore your petitioners pray that your honourable House introduce legislation to grant posthumous pardons to each of these men and that their names shall be included in all official records and memorials to the esteemed soldiers of the Empire Forces who fought bravely and made the ultimate sacrifice for their country in the cause of freedom and justice.[13]

And there it rests. Autumn will become winter and winter spring, and years and decades move on to other centuries. Still the suspicion will remain, the canker still fester, the injustice stay unrighted. For our nation's history is stained by these court martials. The Mother of Parliaments, that self-styled defender of justice, is unmoved, deaf to the questions that will not be hushed. The nation that was later to stand alone against the oppressor, turns its back, content to sweep under the carpet the unsavoury fact that a number of its own were sacrificed for a greater good.

God help us if our children's children face such apathy and self-delusion, if they are ever called to serve in a future and unforeseeable cataclysm, should the whole world ring again to the resonance of war.

References

1. Public Record Office, Kew, ref. ADM 156/24.
2. Moore, William, *The Thin Yellow Line*, Leo Cooper, 1974.
3. Babington, Anthony, *For the Sake of Example*, Leo Cooper, revised edition, 1993.
4. Putkowski, Julian and Sykes, Julian, *Shot at Dawn*, Leo Cooper, 1989.
5. The Royal British Legion, letter to L.G. Sellers, 7 December, 1993 (ref. S2/1810/11).
6. Notice of Motions: 15 June, 1992, no 23. 70 [258].
7. Major, John, Prime Minister, letter from 10 Downing Street to Andrew Mackinlay MP, 16 July, 1992.
8. Major, John, Prime Minister, letter from 10 Downing Street to Andrew Mackinlay MP, 10 February, 1993.
9. The Royal British Legion, letter to L.G. Sellers, 7 December, 1993 (ref S2/1810/11).
10. Mackinlay, Andrew, MP, letter from House of Commons to John Major, Prime Minister, 17 February, 1993.
11. Major, John, Prime Minister, letter from 10 Downing Street to Andrew Mackinlay MP, 27 April, 1993.
12. Pardon for Soldiers of the Great War, 19 October, 1993, pp. 159 and 160.
13. House of Lords Record Office: Parliamentary Debates, [245] Commons, no. 126.

Sources of Research

British Library
Cabinet Office, Historical and Record Section
Commonwealth War Graves Commission
General Register Office, Southport
HMSO
House of Commons, Public Information Office
House of Lords, Record Office
Imperial War Museum: Departments of Documents, Printed Books, Photographs and Sound Records
Law Society
Liddle Collection, University of Leeds
Ministry of Defence (MoD): Historical Section; Records Management; Naval Pay; Pensions and Condition of Service Division; Army Historical Branch; Whitehall Library
National Army Museum
Newspaper Library, Colindale
Office of Population Censuses & Surveys, Southport
Public Record Office, Kew
Royal British Legion
Royal Commission on Historical Manuscripts
Royal Naval College, Greenwich

Bibliography

Babington, Anthony, *For the Sake of Example*, Leo Cooper, revised ed., 1993

Complete Poems of Rupert Brooke, Sidgwick & Jackson, 1939

Herbert, A.P., *The Secret Battle*, Methuen, 1919

Jerrold, Douglas, *The Royal Naval Division*, Hutchinson, 1923

Moore, William, *The Thin Yellow Line*, Leo Cooper, 1974

Pound, Reginald, *A.P. Herbert*, Michael Joseph, 1976

Pratt, Sisson, C., Lieut.-Col. RA, *Military Law*, 'Military Handbooks' (ed. Major-General C.B. Brackenbury), Kegan, Paul, Trench, Trubner, 18th ed., 1910

Putkowski, Julian and Sykes, Julian, *Shot at Dawn*, Leo Cooper, revised ed., 1992

Sellers, Leonard, *The Hood Battalion*, Leo Cooper, 1994

Thurtle, Ernest, *Military Discipline and Democracy*, C.W. Daniel, 1920

Index